Confessions Of A Teenage Gamer

By

Nicolas Cole

D0877747

Copyright © 2016 Nicolas Cole
All rights reserved

Withdrawn

Intro

Acknowledgements

I'll be honest, I never understood the point of having an acknowledgements section. As a reader, I usually skip these pages because they are filled with personal mentions and anecdotes no one could possibly appreciate, let alone understand, except the members of the author's inner circle.

Of course, as it comes time for me to place my own work on the world's bookshelf, my tune has changed. After all, while I may have been the one slaving away at the desk, secluding myself from society seeking peace and quiet to put pen to paper (or fingers to keys), I would be naïve and probably arrogant to think I constructed all of this on my own. So I would like to take a moment to acknowledge the people that not only helped bring this book to life, but helped me grow into the person capable of writing the thing at all. Whether it was the way you listened to me sort through my ideas, or encouraged me during times of self-doubt, just know your gestures did not go unnoticed. Without you, this project (and potentially every project that grows hereafter) would never have gotten done, and I would have spent the rest of my life wondering "what if."

You know who you are. Thank you.

Second — and this is what I believe every author's acknowledgement section should be, if for no other reason than to give permission to all the other artists not yet free from their own debilitating self-doubt — I would like to take a brief moment to acknowledge all of the fears I have in calling this project "complete."

I would like to acknowledge that I have well over 3,000 single-spaced Microsoft Word pages in a folder on my laptop called *Confessions of a Teenage Gamer.* I remember the day I started this project: a Saturday, sometime just after Christmas, 2011. I set myself up in the Columbia College Chicago library with a large green tea (I was unsuccessfully trying to wean myself off coffee), a notebook, and my laptop. The library was mostly empty, everyone still on winter break. I got settled at one of the tables, plugged in my headphones, and proceeded to spend the next however many hours, days, weeks watching old World of Warcraft videos, taking notes in my notebook, writing down as many stories and important moments as I could remember from my journey. I made a list of every server I had ever played on. I made another list of every Horde and Alliance player that had in some way influenced my path. I constructed a timeline from Freshman year of high school to Senior year, trying to pinpoint which months I had reached certain milestones: when I had hit puberty, when I had hit Gladiator, etc. The entire first year of my working on this book was mostly planning, and in my head I constructed a wildly ambitious vision of the final product.

I would like to acknowledge that this book turned out very differently than I had originally imagined.

I would like to acknowledge all the days I couldn't write because I expected this project, my first real project, to be my opus — perfect and loved by all, an instant classic. I would like to acknowledge the other days I couldn't write because I was terrified of what my parents, my siblings, my friends, and everyone in the world would think of my story — and, in a sense, what they would think of "me." I would like to acknowledge the other, other days I couldn't write because I had fallen in love with a girl my senior year of college, and time spent gazing into her eyes was more easily and pleasurably spent than time at my desk alone, reliving my awkward adolescence in extreme detail. And I would like to acknowledge the other, other, other days I couldn't write after we

2

broke up a year later and I was so depressed and exhausted from having written the same chapters over and over again that I considered abandoning the project altogether, never calling myself an "author."

I would like to acknowledge that I never gave up.

I would like to acknowledge that the reason why it has taken me five years to write this is because I haven't wanted to say goodbye. I would like to acknowledge that this story represents my wide-eyed adolescence, and deep down I have been afraid to call it "finished" because that would also mean letting go of the kid that once sat in his computer chair believing he would one day grow up to slay dragons.

I would like to acknowledge that much of my fear of criticism and avoidance in publishing this work has been an attempt to protect that child-like part of me. I would like to acknowledge that I'm glad I didn't publish the first draft, or the second draft, or the third draft, or even the fourth draft, because as much as I'd thought I'd let go of the anger from my adolescence, I hadn't yet — and every time I went back to revise another chapter, all I was really doing was refining the same frustrated, abandoned, unhappy tone. I would like to acknowledge that deep down I always knew something about the writing wasn't right, that I was still writing from a place of hostility instead of reflection. I would like to acknowledge that I still felt like I had something to prove.

I would like to acknowledge the path and all the lessons I had to learn in order for me to get to where I am today, undefined by any sort of "external" success; I mean where I am emotionally. I would like to acknowledge that I forgive my parents and my family for everything that happened, and I would also like to acknowledge that I forgive myself for the pain I put them through and that I take accountability for the fact that I was by no means an easy sibling or child.

I would like to acknowledge that the grueling process of writing and rewriting this book helped me do that.

I would like to acknowledge that there is no more genuine pursuit in life to me than writing. I would like to acknowledge that my measure for success is not in how many copies I sell, or how many awards I win, or how many other authors feed me words of validation. I am only successful if I have shared from my heart without an ounce of apology, standing on my own two feet and confessing my deepest truths with the world.

I would like to acknowledge by that definition, this project was a success.

I would like to acknowledge that five, ten, twenty years from now, I will probably look back on this first book and cringe at all its imperfections. I would also like to acknowledge that immediately following that cringe will be a smile of deep gratitude for having had the guts to do it in the first place.

I would like to acknowledge that nothing I have achieved in my entire life has ever felt as good as the release of this book. And I would like to acknowledge that the real reward is not the finished product, but all the lessons I learned along the way.

And finally, I would like to acknowledge how much I love my family. The fact that they are one of the only topics I could write about until the end of time should stand as a testament to the amount of space I hold for them in my heart. Nothing I write, ever, is in any kind of malice toward them, regardless of what the story may portray or capture emotionally. I believe the love of a family is one of the greatest gifts any human, animal, plant, or energetic being can experience here on earth, and that is why I cannot help myself but to write about it. All of it. Because each one of us knows that love and, if anything, need to be reminded of its depth.

As we prepare to dim the lights, cue the music, and begin the show, I would like to acknowledge how excited I am to share this with you. Nervous. A little sweaty. But excited.

This is everything I am. This is me at my most vulnerable.

I would like to acknowledge that I am ready.

Chapter 1
A Town Called Hypocrisy

I am not the same person I used to be.

For the first 18 years of my life, I lived alone in the bathroom. I taught myself how to beatbox, in the bathroom. I taped the blade of my hockey stick while dreaming of what the NHL would be like, in the bathroom. I would carry my dad's laptop upstairs with me, sit on the toilet, and, because our wireless Internet wouldn't reach from the basement to the third floor of our white-collar mansion, I would open a Word document and start writing, in the bathroom. I would sit there for so long that my legs would go numb and my ass would turn red and my mom would finally come upstairs knocking, "Cole? Are you still in there?" One day, I would become rich and famous and I would build the perfect bathroom: with a tray table that would come out of the wall, and a laptop always charging next to the plunger, and maybe even a mini-fridge nearby with endless bottles of orange juice. How I would ever become rich and famous while on the toilet I had no idea, but my future was certain: it would have to be done from the bathroom.

The majority of my childhood, early adolescence, and formative teenage years were spent undiagnosed with Celiac Disease — a food allergy to the most commonly used ingredient in America, wheat. The bathroom closest to the kitchen was my safe haven after a destructive dinner. The bathroom connected to my bedroom gave me shelter in the middle of the night. The bathroom in the basement is where I kept a nice collection of *Game Informer* magazines for whenever the plague struck and there wasn't enough time to make it upstairs. Hours, days, years of my life were flushed down the toilet as I sat, digging my nails into my thighs, squeezing, heaving, pleading for the pain to be over already, please God, make the diarrhea stop! A bomb would finally release, toilet water would splash up, the smell of death pulsing within four walls, and then all at once a calm would settle, like the rising sun after warfare. I would take a deep breath, and, for half a second, feel relief.

But was it over?

2nd grade: sitting on the alphabet carpet, a warning shot firing from my pants, all the kids plugging their noses and saying, "Who did that?" with me joining them, the best pretender of them all: "Yeah, gross. Whoever did that is gross."

5th grade: raising my hand, asking to be excused to the restroom, only to return twenty minutes later, the whole class knowing; they knew I'd gone number two, not number one, and probably a really bad number two because I'd been gone for so long.

7th grade end-of-the-year picnic: an ice cream social at someone's house, stacking my sundae with intestinal assassins disguised as Oreo cookies (wheat) and graham crackers (wheat). I sat down at the long wooden picnic table beside my friends, my crush just happening to sit opposite of me. She had horizon blonde hair in a ponytail, and big blue eyes that smiled like the open sea. This was it, the perfect opportunity. I was going to ask her what her favorite ice cream was and then see if she wanted to be my partner for the water balloon toss — and when everyone was getting ready to leave is when I'd ask her to be my girlfriend.

Within minutes of my first bite into the sundae, I felt the tide shift. I tried to hold it but couldn't. I quickly abandoned the table and asked one of the chaperones if I could go inside and use the bathroom. She pointed me to the basement, and without seeming too desperate — eager fecal matter poking at my quivering butthole — I thanked her and made a run for it. Stairs vanished in my wake. I reached for the doorknob and before my cargo shorts were even past my knees, a wild splatter exploded into the bowl below. I panted. I winced. I squeezed my face and curled my toes

6

and hated being human because for some reason I was the only child born on the face of this planet who couldn't take a normal poop.

When I was done, at least for the moment, I turned to my left. Where there should have been a nice healthy roll of toilet paper was only a golden rod, empty and alone. Surely there was some toilet paper behind me. Under the sink? In the shower? Please! But no, there was no hope. This was my reality. I considered screaming for help, but then everyone would know my secret — everywhere I went, diarrhea. I wiggled on the toilet seat and shook off what I could, and then gently stood up with my shorts around my ankles and waddled over to the sink. I looked at myself in the mirror. Only me. This would only happen to me. I jumped up into the sink and aimed my ass under the faucet. With my hand scooping water, I wiped my brown remains down the drain.

When I went back upstairs, they had started the water balloon toss without me. At the other end of the lawn I saw her, the love of my life, paired with one of the soccer players — a boy who took normal poops, I was sure. She was laughing, her bright white smile in glimmering braces aimed towards the sky, her head back. I wanted to tell her how beautiful she looked, write her a poem even and leave it by her backpack. One of the parents yelled out, "Cole, do you need a partner?" Everybody looked over, even her. But before I could respond, my stomach dropped again, fear rattling through my body. To my entire 7th grade class I had to publicly admit, "Actually, I'm not feeling so well." My friends called out to me, telling me to stop being lame. With my butt cheeks clenched, I quickly waved goodbye and headed for the back gate. As soon as I hit the street, I ran the whole way home, trying to make it to my own bathroom before the next explosion.

This was my life.

When I wasn't in the bathroom, I was sitting in a doctor's office, listening to another white coat ask me to please describe the consistency of my stools.

"You mean you want me to tell you what my poop looks

7

like?" I said.

"In detail," said the man whose name was finely etched in cursive on the front of his white coat pocket, pens peeking out the top.

I rustled on the padded table, the paper under me crinkling. My mother and father were sitting nearby, hands folded, nodding for me to describe the horror.

"It's bad." I paused, giving him time to jot down the adjective. "It's brown and green, and sometimes orange, even when I don't eat carrots."

"Would you say it's soppy? Mushy?"

"My poop?"

"Yes."

"I don't know, I don't reach in there and touch it."

"Cole," my mother said, "be respectful and tell the doctor what he needs to know."

The balding man nodded for me to continue, pen at the ready with his clipboard.

"Well, don't get grossed out, but it's pretty much like water. It's like mud. Sometimes it's chunky, but not really. It's like I'm peeing from my bottom."

My father gave me a stern, satisfied look. A Catholic look. I had used the appropriate word for my gluteus maximus. We were not allowed to use the word "butt" in this family.

You think I'm exaggerating. I'm not. From the moment I popped out of the womb to my 18th birthday, diarrhea. So much diarrhea. At first, my parents were sympathetic, very reassuring, "We'll figure this out, Cole, don't you worry." They took me to the best doctors, did their own research, organized an assortment of diets for me to try. But with each failed diagnosis they grew more and more frustrated, still wanting to help me, as parents do, but tired of always hearing the same excuse: "I can't. I have a stomach ache."

And it's not like my mom couldn't relate. She had been struggling with the same issues ever since college. After her and my dad got married and my dad became a surgeon, he sent her to top-notch gastroenterologists, had every test under the sun done, and still, no answer to her intestinal problems. She'd grown used to the routine, and had little tolerance for my escapism.

"You can't let this rule your life, Cole," she'd say on the other side of the bathroom door, baiting me to come out. "I go through the same thing. But do I give up? No. I put some toilet paper in my purse and I deal with it."

How did I deal with it?

I stopped eating.

If poop was the problem, then I'd simply stop making it.

My routine was as follows: I would wake up for school, drink two glasses of orange juice for breakfast, skip lunch, come home, skip a snack, go straight to hockey practice, skate up and down the ice with my head pounding in a chant for calories, come home exhausted, wolf down a massive dinner (wheat), run to the bathroom, go to bed, wake up, and repeat the cycle over again the next day. I only allowed myself food when in the proximity of a home toilet. My toilet. Where nobody could hear the sounds of war echoing from my chute.

Don't get it confused — I was not anorexic. This was not some strange aspiration of mine to resemble an emaciated mannequin. If anything, I cursed the invisible man in the sky for not giving me the opportunity to grow. Here He was, showering all my peers with the seeds of manly qualities — changed voices, muskrat mustaches, newborn baby biceps — and what did I get? I got shit.

Which really made pursuing my dreams difficult, as you can imagine. All I wanted, more than anything else in the world, was to play in the NHL and become the captain of the Detroit Red Wings. There, I wouldn't be seen as a fragile boy with diarrhea. I would be a gladiator! I would win championships, meet a Victoria's Secret model, have seven kids, all boys, and coach my own hockey team with all of them on it. And that reality was totally plausible; I could see my dream clear as day every time I would take a seat by myself on the toilet in the bathroom. But then another cramp would settle in, and a bomb would drop below me, and I would wonder when and how that dream would ever become my reality.

It wasn't even a doctor that figured me out. It was my mom, years later. She had been reading some book with a smiling blonde on the cover looking far too excited about a raw head of broccoli, and one afternoon, after much deliberation on her part, she handed me the book and said, "Cole, I think we might be allergic to bread."

"At this point, I wouldn't be surprised," I said with sarcasm. Being allergic to bread sounded ridiculous, like being allergic to air.

"I'm serious. The more I read, the more it all makes sense. It's called Celiac Disease."

Keep in mind, this was back in 2008. The masses didn't know what Celiac Disease was yet, and going gluten-free hadn't become a "trend."

"So no more pizza?" I asked.

"And a lot of other things," she said, informing me of the doom. "Wheat is in almost everything, especially in America. This would mean no more breaded chicken, no more flour tortillas, no more pancakes or brownies or chocolate chip cookies."

The list went on and on, and the longer she talked, the less interested I became. It seemed like my only options for food would be vegetables, rice, and plain chicken.

"I'd rather die," I said.

I was about to leave for college. I could see it now: me

trying to make friends while at the same time explaining the advantages of eating non-wheat based foods.

Less than a month later, groaning from the bathroom in pain, I finally waved the white flag. I decided to try a gluten-free diet for a week and never looked back. My poop was solid, my soul singing the sweet song of solace. For me, life began anew.

You may be asking what this has to do with gaming. I'll tell you exactly what this has to do with gaming. Had I not spent the first 18 years of my life chained to the toilet by a fear of being caught in the real world with the sudden need to release a storm of bowels and no toilet to aid me, I might have grown up "normal." My parents used that word a lot. "It's not normal, Cole, to spend eight hours in front of the computer. It's not normal to have friends over the Internet. It's just not *normal.*"

You know what else isn't normal? Weighing 100 lbs as a senior in high school.

What *was* normal was, well...I suppose we could call it "The American Dream."

My parents tell the story all the time: How they got married right out of college and moved into a dumpy little apartment together. How they had to listen to their cat crunching on cockroaches in the other room. How they used to buy 39-cent boxes of macaroni and cheese because that's all they could afford. How my dad would ride his bike ten blocks to the bus stop, then ride the bus 45 minutes to the hospital, and then stay on-call for 72 hours straight kept awake only by coffee mixed with sheer will. How he would return home to my mother, the singer and performer who was working three jobs to support him through medical school. How they would sit down at the dinner table and before she could even ask, "How was your day?" my dad's face would be in the macaroni and he'd be dead asleep. How for years he had worked his tail off, putting in late hours at the hospital. How he slowly climbed up the ranks of doctors. How he eventually became one of the most sought-after spine surgeons in the country. How he'd acquired wealth beyond his wildest dreams. And how finally, finally, he and my mother had made it.

I grew up in a mansion, to say the least. Our house originally belonged to Dick Portillo — founder of Chicago's famous Portillo's Hot Dogs. My three siblings and I ran laps around the empty house, shouting dibs on whichever bedroom we found first. We got lost on back staircases. We jokingly asked where the butlers were. My parents pointed to the black spheres hidden under the gutters and warned us not to misbehave — there were cameras everywhere. We looked out the sunroom window at the massive pool in the backyard and thought we'd arrived in Disneyland. It was incredible.

Except for the fact that the castle had to be kept clean, and food wasn't allowed upstairs, and water glasses needed coasters because mahogany, Cole, this is mahogany, and where is that nice outfit we bought you, why isn't your hair clean, no gym shoes to church, no hockey sticks in the kitchen, no roller blades in the basement, no TV on weekdays, more studying, practice the piano, oh you already practiced, practice more — I mean the list, my God, there was no end!

It was the town. The town really set the stage for all this. Our neighbors had two bright red Ferraris in their garage — one from 1974 and the other from 2002 — and across the street was a small chateau with a driveway the length of a football field, and almost all the dads were millionaires, and most of the moms spent their afternoons at the country club playing tennis, and every kid was enrolled in accelerated Spanish, accelerated Algebra, accelerated college-prep-look-at-me-I'm-ahead-of-you tutoring, which explains why my parents pushed us to practice the piano, the violin, dress appropriately, watch our mouths, learn proper manners, don't watch TV, study more, excel! It was because of the game! We had to beat the game!

Such a fun game, I mean honestly. Truly. Sincerely, from the bottom of my heart, the most fun game, this game of life. My parents create a character: Me. I do not get to choose my eye color, my skin color, my height, or my bone structure, or even the way I laugh or cry or say certain words like tomayto or tomahto. I get it all from them. They decide where I go to school, what sort of clothes I'm allowed and not allowed to wear, what language is appropriate to be coming out of my mouth, everything, they decide it all. And sure, I can go my own way every once in a while, maybe stare at some boobs on the Internet when they're not looking, say fuck-shit-ass-bitch-cunt-shoo-bee-dee-doo-wop behind closed doors, but all in all, for the first however many years of my time on earth, I have very little control over who I am to become. I am their creation, their evolving work of art.

As if this isn't frustrating enough — not just for me, but children everywhere, I am sure — this game for us was taken to a different level when we moved into what I would call a fairy tale of a suburb. It was as if we were all trapped together in a little plastic bubble. This bubble where everyone was white, nobody was black, *my* son is pre-med, yeah well *my* daughter just got her first *booking agent*, well *we're* going to the *Hawaiian islands* for *Spring Break*, oh that's *so ironic* because *we're* going to the *Hawaiian islands too* but *we're* staying in the *Presidential Suite*, I *see* well *we* have to be back early because *our* youngest son is going to be in *California* competing in *nationals* for *soccer*, oh my *goodness* good for *him* you know *my* youngest son has already been *accepted* to all the top schools on a *soccer scholarship*, wow isn't that just *fantastic* because that reminds me of *my* middle daughter who just got stopped on the *street* and asked if she wanted to model for *Vogue* but we're going to have to *think about it* because she has a full ride to *Harvard* next fall, well isn't that just *terrific* you know *my* oldest son went to Harvard and graduated at the top of his *class* and now he works for *Google*, oh you must be so *proud* just like *I* am of *my* daughter because *she* just accepted a *summer internship* working on the *Republican campaign* for the upcoming *election* and that'll give her a lot of *pull* when she's in *law school* and because my *husband* knows the *Vice President* well you never *know* what could *happen*, no you never *know* and that's exactly how *we* felt when *our* oldest son was *applying* for *college* and *we* thought his resumé needed a little *work* so we signed him up for a few *camps* and now he's teaching *underprivileged children* around the *world* how to speak *English* and is in *direct contact* with a few of the *archbishops* who know the *Pope* and so I mean you just really *never know*, no you really *don't*, life is *funny* that way isn't it, sure *is*.

It was the town, I'm telling you, the town! My parents, their intentions had been sincere. All they wanted was to give us what they never had, opportunities to succeed, options to go wherever we wanted to go, learn whatever we wanted to learn. They chose this little town because, on paper, it was everything and more a parent could give a child: opportunity, safety, privilege. But something changed once the papers had been signed and we'd moved into the mansion, once we started meeting the neighbors and attending the new schools and my parents started to spend more and more time with these elite child creators who obsessed, I mean obsessed to no end, over their children. Suddenly a new game began for us, and it was a game the rest of this little town was addicted to playing.

The name of the game was Success.

In order to achieve Success, there had to be constant communication: your current status in school, how far along are you with the new Beethoven piece, what sort of GPA are we looking at mister, what are your goals? Are you truly aiming for greatness?

This was not a very fun game for me to play, let me tell you —a game entirely dependent upon image, what do you look like, how do you carry yourself, what titles have you collected, do people respect you, do people look up to you, are you ahead of everyone else, are you the perfect embodiment of wealth and privilege, are you an investment showing promising returns? You see, I was none of those things. I was very skinny. I had a concave chest. My teeth were all sorts of jagged and in the middle of my forehead were always one or two pieces of bright and ripe acne. My arms and legs looked like twigs. My laugh was too loud. My clothes never fit and I did poorly in school. I got nervous during tests. I didn't understand the questions. I overthought everything. I was afraid to talk to girls. I never felt like one of the guys. I wasn't good at any sports except hockey. Yes, the way I defended against all my insecurities was through the comforting and grandiose dream that one day I would make it to the NHL. Once there, my father would be proud of me, my mother would be proud of me, and I would finally, finally, feel loved and be at ease with myself because I had reached Success.

This grandiosity, of course, was nothing but a defense mechanism.

But do not think for one second that I did not give it my best effort! I tried to play this game, really I did. I was no naturally God-given character, but I sure as hell tried to be! In the morning, I'd wake up early, extra early, and unload globs of gel into my hands. I'd run my slimy fingers through my hair, like an Italian, straight back. Then I'd spike it. Flick it. Twenty minutes I'd stand there, trying to figure out if I had the credentials to pull off the full spike. Because I really liked the full spike. Especially here in front, see how it's proportionate to my ears? But I just, I don't know. Maybe the flick would be safer. Only the really cool guys did the full spike, and I definitely wasn't that cool. I mean maybe, maybe one day I would be. But not yet. No, I haven't gotten there yet. In fact, I'm not sure I'll ever get there. I'll probably never be good enough. Why even bother.

And then I'd try some more! I'd wear my puka shell necklace from our vacation in Florida, the shells scratching at my bare and tender neck. I'd wear t-shirts from Abercrombie & Fitch with sayings on the front like, "Cultured and Experienced." I'd walk into class right before the bell, swaggering over to my desk and leaning back in my chair the same way all the popular guys did, one arm on the desk, the other arm behind me, my head cocked to the side and my mouth slightly agape. When the teacher called on me, I pretended like I didn't know the answer. Being cool was all about not knowing the answer. At lunch, I'd do laps around the cafeteria, holding my red plastic tray and a small bowl of pasta (wheat). I would maintain this intentionally confused look on my face — *where are my friends, my friends are around here somewhere* — slowly waiting out the lunch period, alone. In math class, the pretty girl next to me would ask, "Does anyone have an extra pencil?" and I'd start rummaging through my backpack trying to find one I hadn't used yet, one with a perfect eraser, she deserved the perfect eraser. I'd say, very eagerly, "Here you go," but she would already be turned toward the soccer player on the other side of her, taking his pencil instead. A pencil that wasn't even sharpened and full of scratch marks and didn't have an eraser at all.

I swear, I tried everything! I took long sips at the water fountain, showing whatever girl was standing behind me that if I could drink water for this long, just imagine how well I could do other more *sensual* things. I stood on the outside perimeter of the "cool kids" circle in gym class, laughing at all their jokes, trying to inch my way in whenever I got the chance. I endured infinity rounds of two-for-flinching. The fat football player next to me, three times my size, would throw a fake punch, I'd flinch in terror, and then he'd slam his fist twice into my bony shoulder, shouting, "Two for flinching, pussy!" But no matter how much I endured, nothing changed for me. No girls admitted their crushes. No guys welcomed me to sit at their lunch table. The only person in the entire school who seemed halfway interested in being my friend was this loud, overweight, gamer kid named Alex.

We sat next to each other during first period Intro to HTML. He had long hair that always reeked of coconut shampoo, and he wore tight fitting polo shirts — so tight you could see, in detail, his stomach rolls underneath. And every day during class he tried to sell me on this new game coming out called the World of Warcraft.

"It's like, imagine jerking off your entire life," he said. "All you know is your hand. You think it's great, maybe throw some of your mom's lotion on there to make it feel all slippery. Then one day, a real live girl comes along, and for some reason, she decides to let you put your penis in her vagina. That's what World of Warcraft is going to be, Cole. Xbox is your hand. World of Warcraft is a vagina."

I thought the game looked stupid. Sitting in front of a tiny computer screen seemed like a downgrade compared to playing Halo on the 72-inch television in our basement. But the real reason I wasn't interested was because Alex wasn't quite who I was looking for. I was looking for someone with social pull. Someone with friends that were hot girls. Someone that could show me, teach

16

me, please, guide me up the ladder so that I could reach Success and beat this game of life!

Here it is: How did I get started playing World of Warcraft? A few weeks into my freshman year of high school, I fractured my spine playing hockey. Not from anything amazing like scoring a game-winning goal while getting checked from behind. I just slipped and fell the wrong way during practice, and ended up with a stress fracture at the bottom of my spine — too small to operate, too big to ignore, no doubt the result of being constantly malnourished. Course of treatment was a bottle of Advil and a Velcro back brace for six weeks.

Suddenly, I had no North Star, no goal I could point to and aim for its achievement, no promise from the future to help me tolerate the present. Instantly, I fell into a dark and destructive depression. I felt lost and without purpose. My grandiosity that one day I would play in the NHL turned to self-hatred — now I would truly never be enough. And to make matters worse, the cure to my injury was being dangled in front of me in the form of my father. My father is a spine surgeon. And in devilish joy, I could hear the heavens cackle at my despair. Here was a man — a man I didn't see very often because he left early in the morning and came home late at night — who could put his holy hands on people's spines and make them walk again. He told stories around the dinner table about the people he'd healed, and to my ears, these were true miracles. My siblings, my grandma, my mom and I, sat close and listened like his disciples. He was, in my eyes, as powerful as God.

Yes, it is all too cosmically brilliant that my hockey injury, the stomach aches, my relentless desire for achievement, my all-too-visceral daily bouts of bathroom-induced depression, and the hermetic symbolism of my father standing as a testament to my left brain and my mother singing songs from my right, concocted a perfect storm of opportunity. There I was, alone and on the toilet with a Velcro back brace around my torso, feeling in me this insatiable drive to become something great in life with no feasible outlet to call my own, when suddenly, this video game appears. Out of nowhere. A world where I could be my own creator, reinvent

Chapter 2
Somewhere I Belong

I knocked on the front door.

Alex lived on the other side of town, where the houses only had one garage, and the driveways were much shorter, and the cars parked in front didn't look fresh out of the dealership. Alex lived with his mom, no siblings, and didn't have a dad — or, at least, he never talked about him.

From deep within the house, a voice called out, "IT'S OPEN." I turned the doorknob and let myself in, holding it open with my foot while I picked my black desktop up from the ground and waved goodbye to my mom.

Alex's living room had a small TV, a two-person couch, and a single rocking chair. I followed his voice — "I'M DOWN HERE." Hanging on the walls of the tight hallway were little framed pictures — Alex in a baby bonnet, Alex in his pirate costume for Halloween, Alex holding a red Gameboy color on the couch next to his Grandma.

"Where are you?" I called out, not knowing my way around.

"WHERE DO YOU THINK I AM," he shouted, and I followed the sound down the three stairs and into their one-room basement — Alex's bedroom.

The smell hit me as soon as I opened the door. Packed into the four tiny walls of Alex's room were three buzzing desktops, a swamp of stray chords, several boxes of pizza, and three pairs of eyes staring at their computer screens. There was a horrific aroma of burnt body odor lingering in the air. In many ways, it smelled just like a hockey locker room. And as sour the stench, it felt like home.

Alex and two other kids spun around in their computer chairs. Alex, wearing only his boxers with a fan on his desk blasting him in the face at full speed, shouted, "Welcome to the LAN party!"

I'd never seen anything like it. In the corner he had an old TV with every console imaginable hooked up to the front: Xbox, GameCube, PS2, Dreamcast, Playstation, Nintento64, the original Nintendo, even a Sega Genesis. In the other corner was a mattress on the floor, no bedframe, with one stray sheet crumpled in the middle. Pushed up against the right wall was a long table with two leather desk chairs sitting in front of two black desktop computers. All over the walls were half-naked female video game characters from Final Fantasy, posing provocatively in armored bikinis.

Alex's room was everything my bedroom had never been allowed to be. He didn't have designer window treatments or brand new carpeting or chic bookshelves that leaned at an angle against the wall. But he had freedom. The freedom to hang posters and keep a lava lamp next to his bed. And for that, I was jealous.

Alex pointed to his two friends sitting at the card table in the middle of the room. He said, "Cole, meet the crew."

Scott was a slightly overweight kid with short disheveled hair. His lips were coated orange from fistfuls of Cheetos and on his lap was a plastic plate of pizza, some of the greasy cheese falling off the side and staining his cargo shorts. Peter, on the other hand, wore black dress shoes, blue jeans, and a light blue collared shirt, tucked in, with a black belt and silver buckle. He sat straight up, perfect posture, and ate the pizza next to his keyboard with a fork and knife. His hair was neatly combed to one side, and his glasses were pushed close to his face.

I looked at the three of them. They were not the friends I had originally set out to find. But they played World of Warcraft. And as a gesture of introduction, they raised their cans of Diet Coke to me. Whether I liked it or not, I was one of them.

As I set my computer down beside the open chair, Alex reached inside the mini-fridge next to him. He grabbed two Diet Coke's, threw one to me and said, "Let me know when you're all set up. I'll help you create your WoW character." Before the sentence was even out of Alex's mouth, he was placing his headphones over his head and turning back towards his computer.

"WoW?" I asked, not understanding the lingo.

Alex paused, holding one earphone out over his ear, and eyed me suspiciously. "World of Warcraft?" he said slowly, waiting for the abbreviation to sink in.

"Got it," I said, nodding with enthusiasm.

Alex let out a deep breath. "Christ. I have so much to teach you."

Scott and Peter started laughing, their eyes glued to their computer monitors.

I took my seat in the provided foldable lawn chair and started to assemble my rig. From my backpack I pulled out my tiny twelve-inch monitor, my keyboard, mouse, mouse pad, and a few bags of potato chips — my contribution to the party, stolen from our pantry at home. From my pocket, I pulled out a tiny scrap of paper with my dad's credit card information on it. Playing World of Warcraft required a monthly fee, but Alex had assured me it was for a good cause. "Imagine how much you already spend on video games. $50 per game, a new game every, what, month or two? Probably more? This is $15 a month instead of $50, for an even better game. Trust me, if anything, I'm saving you money."

I had regurgitated the same script to my dad, word for word. I spoke of dollars saved and a better gaming experience. My dad wanted to know how I could prove that his credit card

mouth like braces on a teenager. He had skinny limbs, and long veins like ropes. He had lime-green hair that stuck straight up, as if he'd been electrocuted, and his face lacked all the determination of the Night Elf. This Troll was, by every definition, a breathing metaphor for everything I already hated about myself.

"I really don't think this is the character for me," I said.

Alex disagreed, and lectured on the benefits of playing such an unpopular class. "Hardly anyone is a Shaman," he said, as if this was supposed to make me feel better. "Supply and demand, Cole. Be the demand."

In an attempt to get on Alex's good side and further our friendship, which would ensure my fruitful future in the game, I heeded his advice.

"Ok," I said, after selecting my Troll's hair and skin color.

"You ready?" said Alex.

"I think so."

"What did you name your character?"

"Peragus."

"You make that up?"

"It's a planet from Star Wars."

Scott laughed. "He'll fit right in," he said, taking a long swig from his Diet Coke.

"He sure will," said Alex. "Cole, hit the enter key."

I hit Enter and the loading screen appeared.

As I waited to appear inside the game, Alex, suddenly very serious, said, "You know this game is going to change your life."

I popped the tab on my own Diet Coke, something I never drank, and took a sip. The fizzy black liquid tickled my lips and tongue. We weren't allowed to have soda at our house.

"What do you mean?" I asked.

"Ten years from now, do you really think you're going to care about anybody from our shitty little high school? You're not. They're all a bunch of fake fucks. Think about it. *He said this, she said that.* It's just one big shitstorm of drama."

Alex turned towards his computer and pointed right at his screen.

"You want lifelong friends? This is where you're going to find them."

I burst out laughing.

"Inside the computer?" I said.

"In the World of Warcraft," he said.

"It's true," said Peter, spinning around in his chair, looking at me and pushing his glasses up his nose.

I set down my Diet Coke.

"No offense, but I really can't see myself becoming friends with someone on the Internet."

"I know," said Alex. "Before I started playing Everquest, I said the same thing. But you wait, Cole. Couple weeks from now, you'll be doing a quest with some kid, and you'll start talking about random shit like what quest you should do next, and then you'll get bored and you'll tell him that you want some pizza, and he'll say that he wants pizza too, and you'll both start debating which frozen pizza tastes the best. And then before you know it you'll be talking every day, and you'll know he has two brothers, and a sister, and always fights with his mom, and his dad is never home, and he'll know the same shit about you, and you'll find yourself logging online more for the friendship than the game itself."

"Alex," I said, shaking my head, "how am I going to

become friends with someone I've never met before?"

"You'll see," he said.

The house phone beside Alex's computer started to ring.

Ring.

Ring.

He pressed the speakerphone button and said, "What."

"Alex, I'm making dinner. What would you boys like?"

It was Alex's mom, upstairs, easily within yelling range.

"Tell her to order more pizza," said Scott.

"More pizza, Mom," said Alex.

"Sweetie, we already ordered pizza today. Can't you have something else?"

"Frozen pizza," said Scott.

"Fuck that," said Alex, and his mom squealed, "Alex! Watch your mouth!"

He ignored her. "Mac and cheese, Mom."

"Let me see if we have any, you might have eaten it all," she said.

"Fatass," Scott whispered.

Alex gave Scott the finger.

"Mom, Cole just got here."

Alex's mom spoke louder into the phone, as if to reach me. "Hi, Cole!"

With good manners, I spoke up. "Hello, Mrs. Wilcox."

"Is mac and cheese alright for you too?"

"Sure, thank you."

"What about Peter, is he still down there?"

"Yea, I'm here. Mac and cheese is cool."

"Ok!" she said.

"HEY, WHAT ABOUT ME," yelled Scott.

"Lots of cheese, Mom," said Alex, and then he hung up.

Thirty minutes later, four steaming hot plates of bright gold mac and cheese (wheat) came parading down into Alex's room, topped with extra slices of melted American cheese. Alex opened his mini fridge and passed out another round of Diet Cokes. Alex's mom handed each of us our own plate, tiptoeing over our chords and power strips. I pushed my keyboard forward to make room for my dinner, and proceeded to stuff my face along with the rest of them, one hand clutching my fork, the other resting on the left-hand side of my keyboard, controlling my Shaman.

It was gaming in its purest form — nothing but junk food, caffeine, and the World of Warcraft.

Alex, Peter, and Scott were different than the other kids at our school. They didn't ask me if the Holocaust had called about a missing body — a joke I often heard from guys in my gym class about my bony arms and frail figure. They didn't make fun of me for the Velcro brace I had to wear around my back. The only thing they cared about was whether or not I was going to take the World of Warcraft seriously. If it didn't have to do with the game, it didn't matter. This was an unspoken code I was quick to pick up on.

"Peter, you got any potions?" said Alex.

"Two Minor Health and two Minor Mana."

"Dammit, I need Agility Elixirs."

"I think Scott has some."

"Scott?"

"Shut the fuck up, you still owe me for the cloak Enchant."

"I paid you back!" yelled Alex.

"You didn't pay me shit."

"You said five Silver. I gave you five Silver."

"No, you gave me three Silver and a stack of Linen and said it was worth the difference. Linen is 50 Copper a stack on the Auction House right now you cheap fuck."

For the entire night, all the way until 3:30 in the morning, I listened attentively, trying to interpret this strange new language. They spoke of Stamina Buffs and Intellect Enchants, group compositions and dungeon requirements. They dreamed aloud of the day they would all reach Level 60 and what guilds they hoped to join. Alex was right — this was no ordinary video game. This was a community, a secret society, and I was soon to become an earnest member.

The next morning, we were jolted awake by Alex's alarm at 7:30 a.m. We'd barely gotten four hours of sleep. I was curled up underneath the card table on his crumb-covered floor, no sleeping bag, using my backpack as a pillow and my sweatshirt as a blanket.

"Time to get up!" Alex said, reaching into his mini fridge for a Diet Coke to start the day.

"What time is it?" I said, my eyes squinting to find a clock.

"I JUST WANT TO SLEEP," Scott groaned.

"Level 60 isn't going to happen on its own!" Alex yelled, and plopped himself down in his computer chair.

"Studies show that the human body needs at least seven hours of sleep per night to function effectively," said Peter, putting on his glasses.

"I don't give a shit what some virgin from Harvard says. You all need to decide how badly you want to succeed in the World of Warcraft," said Alex. "And I don't know about you pussies, but I want Level 60 really fucking badly. Four hours of sleep is more than enough. Now get up."

Scott and Peter nodded and dragged themselves up off the floor and into their computer chairs, logging back into the game. Alex looked over at me and said, "You going to earn yourself a ballsack today, Cole? Or are you just going to lay there like a noob."

My back ached from the night spent without a bed. My mouth tasted like pennies, and behind my eyes was a dull pounding — either from a lack of sleep or the ten straight hours I'd spent looking at a computer screen the night before. In my stomach, a storm was brewing from last night's macaroni and cheese, and in my left wrist was a sharp pain from the strict position it had held on the keyboard. With the sun blasting through Alex's tiny window, all I wanted was to pull my sweatshirt over my head and go back to sleep.

But I didn't. I couldn't. As tired as I was, for the first time in months I was happy. I'd found a group of friends, no matter how strange. I had a list of quests to complete, levels to achieve. In the World of Warcraft, I had found somewhere to belong.

I pulled myself up and took a seat at my computer.

Chapter 3
Breathing

A voice came over the intercom, projecting itself into every room of our mansion — the bedrooms, the living room, the parlor, the turret, the basement, they all had intercoms on the walls. The voice was my father's, and rang throughout the house like God.

"Dinner is served. I repeat, dinner is served. All children, report to the kitchen immediately."

Mom, Dad, Grandma, Brooke, Thomas, Donald, and me, all took our seats around the circular wooden dinner table. Above our heads hung a crystal chandelier.

"Bless us, oh lord, for these, our gifts, which we are about to receive, from thy bounty, through Christ, our lord, Amen."

Fingers to forehead, chest, right shoulder to left shoulder, "In the name of the Father, Son, Holy Spirit, Amen."

And then our nightly family ritual began:

"So this morning," my mother said, "I saw the most *incredible* episode of *Oprah*."

Tonight was barbequed ribs, my dad's recipe, cooked to perfection by our Polish sitter, nanny, and chef, Lidia. I started cutting mine, fork and knife. Brooke, two years younger than me, picked hers up with her hands and gnawed off a huge chunk of flesh, the sauce coating the left side of her cheek. Thomas and Donald, six and seven, transformed their forks into laser guns by pointing them at each other and adding sound effects, "Pew pew,

Around the table we went, the parents asking the children about their days, what was on the horizon, what we needed to plan for, how we were going to measure Success.

But not without laughter! Such an amazing family this was, with music always ringing out, a theatrical cast as we loaded our plates into the dishwasher. "Sing it again!" I would wail in an operatic voice, Brooke joining me in the fun with a harmony, Thomas and Donald chasing each other around the kitchen wielding Nerf guns, my mother in tears laughing with her children, the most entertaining children in the whole world, while my father took a wet paper towel to the marble kitchen island and shook his head wondering where on earth his serious, down-to-business genes had gone, and why none had seemed to manifest in his offspring. And then my father would quickly vanish from the scene, only to emerge thirty seconds later wearing a chapeau or a bonnet or a safari hat found from the hallway closet. We would laugh, *Dad, you always do this*, he would laugh, *what, what's so funny, this is my normal hat*, and on and on we would go, performing, performing, performing.

The most magnificent family you've ever seen, truly. We joked often there should be a television show based on us. We believed ourselves to be that fantastic.

But the whole charade killed me! I mean, I loved it, don't get me wrong; there is no greater pleasure in life than for your mother or your only sister to share with you the most joyous sound of approval — laughter. But, dare I say, this was not my true, authentic voice showing up for dinner every night? That behind this mask of comedy breathed a quiet destruction?

It's true! I loved all the creative freedoms this ongoing performance offered me — which was precisely the problem. Notice, I did not say "freedom," I said "creative freedom." As long as what I was saying was part of a scene, a joke, oh well then of course you can share that, Cole! We would never want you to suppress your creativity! So for example: if I wanted to tell my father and mother that I had just started playing this really cool game called World of Warcraft, and it was teaching me some really

40

interesting vocabulary words, and I loved the way it challenged my brain strategically, well, as long as I did so in a funny voice, as part of a comedic scene, maybe even got up from the table to give action to my "creative expression," you know, to paint the portrait that who was speaking was this nerdy kid who only cared about playing video games, not me, no, not me at all, well then, then my mother and father might not think it to be the most enthralling or entertaining monologue but they certainly wouldn't be upset! Because it was a joke! I was just kidding around! Ha ha. Get it? Don't *worry*, Mom and Dad, I don't *actually* feel like that. I'm *creatively expressing* the feelings of *that kid*, who is by no means *me*.

But, but, if I were to say, at the dinner table, from the deepest concaves of my heart, "Mom, Dad, today I learned something really cool about myself and I learned it inside the World of Warcraft," well, we might still be sitting at that dinner table this many years later! My mother and father going on and on and on about how I was being rebellious, I was defying them, a video game is not a genuine pursuit in life, Cole, and I should, oh this is the real kicker, I should *watch my mouth*.

Watch my mouth! What exactly does that mean? How confusing for a child — a mask of "creative expression" giving him the ability to say just about anything that comes to mind, but remove the mask, speak from the heart, and suddenly he is acting out, he is defying his parents, he is out of line. He. Not what he is saying. *He*. The boy himself and all that he is, is *wrong*.

Does it come to anyone's surprise then that all through my adolescence I associated my voice, my authentic truth in this world, with the comedic mask I wore at the dinner table? Yes! Give me approval! I am funny! I am hilarious! It's all an act! Don't worry! Nothing I am saying is true! For your love, I will be exactly who you want me to be!

Oh, well doesn't that just explain everything.

Six months into my journey within the World of Warcraft, Scott, Peter, and Alex grew bored and quit — but not me. The game

41

had offered me far too many reasons to stay: rewards, achievement, *validation*. Instead of quitting with them, I decided to create myself anew. This time, I would create myself not as I was, but the image of who I wanted to become. I wanted to have an intimidating swagger. I wanted to deal obscene amounts of damage.

Hiding away in my bedroom, my hands took to my keyboard.

I chose a brand new World of Warcraft server and sought to recreate myself. Something menacing. Something people would remember.

I was an Undead Mage, and my name was Cackle.

And what an interesting name — to laugh, to screech, guffaw! I had always been a rather loud child. Just a few months after being born, actually, I screamed so loud and so often that I burst a vocal chord. My mother was holding me while I wailed when, all of a sudden, silence. My little eyes went wide and I looked at her like I'd just lost my soul. I opened my mouth but nothing came out. Just the faint whisper of effort.

And how ironic that my mother is a voice teacher! How, all while growing up, she had tried to teach me how to sing, give me her voice, but I refused—I couldn't accept it. I had to find mine. Mine, Mom. I had to know myself.

And how fascinating that in the World of Warcraft, the voice of each player, for the most part, was conveyed through text. It was all writing. My words, my punctuation, my sentence structure and rhythm of language created an image in the mind of the other person of what sort of boy was in control of the character.

So, ha, do you know what I did? You'll love this. I created myself to be loud as fuck! In search of a voice? Never! I wasn't lost — what a joke. I was found! So fucking found. I was going to be an incredible Mage and I was going to be e-famous and honestly, I was going to be such an absolute superstar that I would have to set aside time every day to talk to my fans, my followers, the players that would eagerly await my arrival online and immediately message me:

[Fanboi] whispers: Omg Cackle you're so fucking amazing, you're probably the best Mage I've ever seen, ever in this game. Do you think you could teach me? I'll be your personal assistant, for free. Whatever you need, done. I'll make your Mage water for you. Not that you need someone to make you water. I'm sure your water is delicious. Probably better than any water I'd be able to make. But I'd be willing to bet you get tired of making your own water, and you could teach me how you like it. Maybe you like it chilled. I could chill it for you. Anything to be like you, Cackle. You're my hero.

My God, what a brilliant plan! Cackle would be the shield behind which I would hide while I went on this journey of self-discovery. I would live behind my persona. Cackle would be the most overconfident, aggressive, sarcastic teenager to ever grace the World of Warcraft, guaranteeing me the world's hatred and thus, protecting me from the verbally vicious community found in online gaming. See, by doing it *on purpose,* I would see the rejection coming *ahead of time,* meaning I could prepare myself for it and avoid it altogether. Other players would think *Cackle* was annoying. They would wish *Cackle* would drink bleach and die. They would call *Cackle* a faggot because *Cackle* didn't know when to shut the fuck up. Not Cole. No, not the boy sitting in his computer chair, desperately trying to find his authentic voice. Cole would remain safe, the brilliant mastermind behind this fictional character, manipulating people to think that *Cackle* was the lost adolescent. And how funny. Ha ha.

This self-preservation strategy, coincidentally, was also the warfare strategy of the Mage. The name of the game for a Mage was to avoid the need to defend by killing the other player before they had the chance to kill you.

I did this very well.

And it makes sense where a lot of this was coming from. I mean, I spent all day at school, sitting quietly in my imitation

43

marble desk, tolerating the teachers and the assignments and the students and the dances — homecoming was three weeks away and I kept thinking I might ask this one girl, or maybe that one, or maybe her, right over there, but then I decided no, I shouldn't put her in that sort of position. My mother had always said, "Treat girls with respect." I should be a gentleman. And inferior gentlemen don't say to beautiful girls, "Would you like to go to homecoming with me?" because then she, the girl, would be put in an awkward position, forced to say the words out loud, "Cole, I already have a date, and like, no offense, but I'm a little out of your league," which I got, totally understood, that's just how the cookie crumbles. She was up there enjoying the first bite, the best bite, the first bite of the cookie is always the best, and I was down here with the crumbs, which were wheat, and gave me diarrhea, every day for all eternity. Better to just save us both the trouble and not ask her at all.

My sophomore year class schedule was mind-numbing: Chemistry, Algebra 2, French 2, U.S. History, English, blah blah; every class and every assignment required the memorization of worthless information holding no applicable value other than to correctly answer a multiple choice question on the day of the exam. I signed up for the Competitive Sports Gym Class because I wanted something during my school day that was actually fun. Competitive Sports Gym Class didn't turn out to be much fun. On the first day, the gym teachers, who were also the football coaches, made us go through a series of tests to gauge our athletic ability: push-ups, sit-ups, stuff like that, to make sure teams were fair and balanced. And it's not like I wasn't athletic. But one of the tests involved a weight scale connected to a bar, and you had to curl the bar so the scale could measure how strong you were and, of course, since this is how guys are, everyone stood in a big fucking circle and watched in awe as football players curled like ninety pounds and tennis players curled like sixty five, and then everyone cackled, I mean cackled their asses off when it was my turn and I could only curl twenty-five pounds. The vein running along my nonexistent bicep looked like it was going to explode, I was trying so hard. It hurt my wrists to curl that much, never before having curled in my entire life, but I kept curling anyway because I wanted them to stop laughing at me, wanted to prove that I too was a male, worthy of acceptance. One of the gym teachers made a note on his clipboard and said, "Looks like it's time to hit the gym, huh Cole." My response was drowned out by the sound of guys punching each other, laughing, yelling "I call Cole is on your team; no we don't want him; well dammit, we don't want him either!" When my turn at the curling station was over, I went to stand in the back of the circle, hoping to just sort of vanish into thin air and never come back.

But oh the joy I felt arriving back home, landing in my computer chair, taking aim at everyone on the Internet!

It was a joke, I swear. One big, outlandish, gut-wrenching joke. That was what made it so great. Cackle was — Christ, how do I even explain it...Cackle was such an interesting character, that kid you always wondered about, lurking in the shadows, living at the bottom of the barrel; I'm talking insecurities like you wouldn't believe, which I didn't have. I mean I did, I had some. But not like Cackle-bad. I was the one in control here, making other players *think* that behind the keyboard was this terrified kid, terrified that the whole world was watching his every move, criticizing his walk, side to side, how he dressed, too much cargo, why is he here, he shouldn't be here, the bed-head hair, the weird smile, the dainty little fingers that...Did anyone ever tell you that the size of your middle finger reflected the size of your penis? Someone told me that once, on the bus, I think it was in 6th grade. This girl said, "Hey Cole, hold up your hands," and I did as I was told, and then her and her friend and the whole backseat basically started cackling, and I said, "What," looking at my hands, turning them every which way, trying to find the problem, and she said, "It's nothing." And then the guy next to her, the guy they all swooned over, said, "A big middle finger means you have a big dick," and I nodded and turned around and proceeded to spend the next however many years examining my and the rest of the population's middle fingers, trying to determine if mine was big or small because that's really important to know, which led to many, many sessions in the bathroom with a ruler, in front of the mirror, measuring my finger, measuring my penis, measuring soft, measuring hard, measuring on different days, measuring in the morning versus at night, measuring right before a shower, right after a shower, in different temperature settings, measuring in comparison to household objects — *See, now beside this toothbrush, I would say I'm actually quite thick, but in comparison to that shampoo bottle, I'm microscopic.* I made sure to tackle the issue from every possible angle, compiling data and then cross-referencing previous months' measurements, hypothesizing about foreseeable growth in the future, being honest on good days, rounding up on bad ones, looking at graphs on the Internet, printing off these weird charts with these different penis sizes drawn on them so you could put the page right on your desk, or wherever, and lay your penis over the drawings to see exactly how big you were, except they must not have been drawn to scale because according to that, I was sporting one of the largest hoses a fireman could carry, and I knew that couldn't have been right because of what I saw on screen, in the videos, with the girls and the mascara and the "God I just love your big dick," a cocktail of saliva dripping down their chins. It just didn't match up. Sometimes, I would pause right in the middle just to compare video frames, deciding that aha! From this angle, his penis does look pretty large, but look here, right here we kind of look like we have the same penis, and she's loving it, really loving it, look at her loving it, and if she's loving that then she'll definitely love this, and I would look down at what I was holding in my hand, and then they, the naked people on my screen, would switch to a different position and all of a sudden, nope, my penis definitely does not stick out that far, and I would get really upset, really worried, actually, about how this was all going to go down later in life, what the girl would say, what she would think of me. I sort of imagined it going down like this: we'd be, well, anywhere really, I had quite the imagination, but somewhere plausible, like an airplane. Her and I would be sitting next to each other, me by the window, her in the middle seat, and she'd say, "Oh my gosh, what a packed flight," and I'd say something in the tone of a Frank Sinatra, "Isn't it always?" And she'd give me one of those flirtatious little half-smiles that would warrant chatting it up for a bit while we waited for the flight attendant to finish her spiel about safety and seatbelts and how these 4x4 floatation devices would somehow save our lives if the airplane were to crash. During takeoff, I'd tell the girl beside me that I needed to close my eyes because this part always makes me feel really sick, I'm fine once we're up in the air,

I just need to get through the roller coaster feeling where I think I'm going to throw up, which she understands, she's the same way, we're perfect for each other like that. And to her left across the aisle is this little old lady who falls asleep the moment they turn off the fasten seatbelt signs, which we laugh about, how cute she is, aww. And then out of nowhere, she (and I'm telling you, the girl sitting next to me is a twelve out of ten, green eyes, dirty blonde hair, really dirty, as in mostly brunette but with a hint of summer vacation) reaches over and starts rubbing the outside of my jeans where I keep the goods, and the first thing she says is, "I want to see it, I bet it's huge." I deflect by pulling her in to kiss me, the whole airplane disappearing from the moment. Before I know it, she's unbuttoning my pants for the first time, this is my first time, it's always my first time — in the forest, on her parents' bed, in a train station bathroom, always the first time — and everyone on the plane is asleep, dead asleep, nobody is going to wake up. She peels apart the zipper of my jeans as if opening the golden gates to a great kingdom, and there's this little lump there, which she starts rubbing, saying, "Looks like I found the top," rubbing more, "It's so thick," rubbing more, "I want it right now." And during all of this I'm just hoping and praying that between the last time I measured and now, somehow I'd grown two, three, seven more inches. And then she pulls down my pants and underwear, only to realize that what she'd thought was just the tip is actually the whole thing, and it's not huge, and it's not thick, and even in my fantasy she leans away and says, "You know, I'm pretty tired too," and then goes to sleep, joining everyone else on the plane in the collective dream, leaving me there, alone, exposed on the airplane, knowing that as soon as we land she'll tell all her friends, who are connected around the world to very powerful people, and it'll probably end up on the news — "This just in, Cole has a tiny penis" — and everyone at school will find out, and it'll follow me for the rest of my life, where I'll forever be a virgin because what girl could possibly find pleasure in this tiny, little, middle finger.

…..

…..

…..

Ha, ha. That's what I was making everyone on the Internet think.

Cackle was that kid.

Not me.

Cackle.

Which caused an interesting thing to happen. The more time I spent as this persona, Cackle, the more he began to bleed into my real life. A whole new kid started showing up to class.

I blurted out answers without raising my hand. I responded to math questions with absurd guesses: "17 billion! 36 trillion! Ha ha! I'm so funny!" I kept a list of how many times girls, the annoying ones standing at the front of the room trying to give their speeches on George Washington or photosynthesis, said the word 'like,' and then at the end of their presentations when they said, "So like, does anyone like, have any like, questions?" I would raise my hand and, not even knowing my name, they would call on me by saying "You," as in, "You in the back," and with an odd new timbre ringing from my vocal chords, a timbre only cultivated through hours of linguistic warfare over the Internet, I would say, "Throughout your presentation, you said the word 'Like' approximately one hundred and eighty-seven times. How does that make you feel?" And the girl, the one who had the perfectly straight blonde hair and a summer dress with matching shoes and a headband that was a sunflower and who never would have said a word to me ever in her entire life, would flare up in fury and start yelling, "Are you serious? Like, that's your question? Do you have any idea like how rude you are? Oh my God, like, Mr. Preston? This is like, totally inappropriate." And I, Cackle, this character that had found his way out of the World of Warcraft and into a desk chair in the back of a high school classroom, arms crossed, legs sprawled, would smile wide as wide could be.

Teachers started calling home. "Cole has been disturbing

48

the class lately. Cole doesn't seem to feel the need to raise his hand. No, his classwork is fine — clearly he's an intelligent boy. He just seems to be looking for attention. Is everything alright at home?"

While on the phone, my mother would look over at me, both of us at the kitchen table enjoying a muffin (wheat), a piece of carrot cake (wheat), or some other delicious after-school treat Lidia had baked (wheat), and my mother would say, her eyes locked on mine, "Cole was being disruptive?" I would raise my eyebrows and shrug my shoulders, totally innocent. Right back, my mother would do the same, shrugging her shoulders, rolling her eyes, these *academics,* always trying to get us *artists* to conform.

"No, no, that doesn't sound like my son," she would say, very sure of herself and her parenting techniques. "He's sitting right here, and he says that's not how it happened. He says he didn't mean to be disruptive. He was just trying to ask a question. It's hard, you know, being in a class with that many students. If anything, I admire my son for having the guts to speak up!"

My mother always gave me the benefit of the doubt. I exploited this masterfully. Until eventually, the calls became so frequent that my parents, my mother mostly, was forced to reconsider her assumptions and take action.

"Cole, we're taking you tomorrow to see a specialist."

"I always knew I was special."

The void between Cole and Cackle was gone now. I was he and he was I.

My parents were not entertained.

"We think you might have what's called ADD. Do you know what that is?" my mother asked, very calm, but very serious.

My father sat nearby, devastated. Never in a million years would he have guessed that his son, his oldest son and heir to his throne, would have been born with a disorder. He shook his head, avoided eye contact, looked like he was about to cry. There would be no cure. I would be put on debilitating medication. I would spend the rest of my life in a wheelchair. I would probably have to live in the basement; yes, he would have to build me a special room in the basement, with handlebars along every wall so that I could grip them as I moved about. He would have to pull a few strings, talk to a few of his CEO friends, "One day, you're playing catch in the backyard with your son, and the next, boom, God hits you with this, you know?" His friends would put their hands on his shoulders and say, "Don't worry, we'll get through this." They'd band together and get me a job at *Jewel Osco*. I would be a bagger. Orange juice down the conveyer belt — good job, Cole! Orange juice into a plastic bag — there you go! Orange juice in plastic bag goes to the paying customer — "Tank yew foar shawping at *Jewul Awsco*, have a gwate day!"

"Mom, I don't have ADD," I said, not an ounce of hesitation in my voice.

"Cole, I know how this must feel, but the first step is going to be admitting that maybe you have a little trouble staying focused."

"You've got to be kidding me."

My Dad, overcome with emotion, jolted forward.

"THIS ISN'T EASY FOR ANY OF US!"

Cut to: Doctor's Office.

[Hot Doctor]: "So, I understand you're here for an evaluation?" she said.

[Mom]: "Yes, yes we are."

My mother was sitting in the tiny chair in the corner, hands folded neatly on top of her purse, her very expensive purse, with her hair freshly highlighted, and her brand new black boots matching her outfit, and her keys, so many keys, she had a lot of responsibilities clutched in her hands, and her diamond studded cross necklace around her neck, one of many, part of a collection, proving devotion to the Catholic church.

I sat up on the crinkly white paper on the squishy examination table. I was wearing sweatpants. I hadn't showered in two days. My gym shoes were three years old and very dirty. My mother tried often to buy me new shoes, but that would have involved me leaving the house and going to the mall. My shirt was wrinkled. I'd worn it several times this week. Not to school. After school. This was my comfy shirt. Nike. Black. "Just Do It" in big white letters on the front. And my necklace was of Saint Nicolas. I had no idea who that was. Or what he stood for. But it was a birthday present. From my mom. And necklaces made me look cool.

[Hot Doctor]: "Cole, I'm going to ask you a few questions."

They were boring questions.

Did I ever tell you about the time...? Ok. So in Second Grade we all had to write a paragraph about something we loved. I wrote about hockey. I always wrote about hockey. Then we had to draw a picture of what we wrote in the box provided above it. And I drew myself, obviously, stick figure, skates, hockey stick, hockey net, the whole thing. After Miss Harper checked our paragraphs for spelling errors, we were supposed to take a black pen and go over the pencil and make it look all professional because they were going to be hung around the class. I picked up my pen and started with the first word. Then I got bored and did the last word of the paragraph. Then I did some words in the middle because why not? Then whatever letters I felt like doing next, sometimes not even finishing the word, the first three letters in black pen, the last two still in pencil. And my teacher, checking to make sure we were doing it right, came and looked over my shoulder and said, "Cole? How's it going?" I held up my paper, proudly showing that I was halfway done. My paragraph was schizophrenic: half in grey pencil, half in black pen, no rhyme or reason to what I was doing, but to me it made perfect sense. She said, "Why don't you go over the words in order?" and pointed to the second word of my paragraph, which I'd yet to trace with my black pen. I looked at her, somewhat bothered

51

as to why she was questioning my method, and I said, "They're all going to be colored in at the end anyways, why does it matter how I get there?" She called home that night and suggested to my parents that I had a learning disability.

[Hot Doctor]: "Which subjects in school would you say are your strengths?"

That reminds me: I learned how to read in the front seat of my mom's minivan.

We were driving to the grocery store, down 55th street. She was about to take the exit towards Ogden, when all of a sudden I looked up and saw a STOP sign. I knew it was a STOP sign. Which meant we had to STOP!

"Mom!"

"What!"

"That says STOP!"

"It does!"

"And, and, AND, and THAT says 55th street! Which MEANS we're on 55th STREET!"

"You're reading!"

"AND, and THAT says RENTAL, and THAT says CHEVY, and THAT says REPUP, REPUBUB, REPUBLICAN!"

In an instant, the whole world opened up to me. Everything I read conveyed a message. It felt so personal, almost like the universe was speaking to me and me only. Before, the world had felt so ambient and elusive. But now, my blindfold was off. I saw how words gave human beings direction, told them where to go and what was what. To read was to understand. Which meant — and yes, as a five year old, this was my first thought — that to write was to hold power in the world.

[Hot Doctor]: "Do you have any idea what you'd like to

study in college? What you'd like to pursue as a career?"

I once tried to host a neighborhood *Yu-Gi-Oh* tournament in my backyard.

I was twelve. I got all my siblings on board. They helped me clean the whole house. We posted signs from the front door to the basement with arrows for the participants to follow. I set up as many tables as I could find: card tables, wooden coffee tables, our second dining room table from the storage room. I dug through closets of toys for an old, bright red, plastic cash register, and stocked it with my own allowance money — in case we needed change. I set my sister up in the basement with it and told her that she was to handle the finances. Unwilling to pay her for her labor, I allowed her to set a tip jar beside the cash register where she might earn a little something for her efforts. She spent an hour making a very fancy sign and taped it to the front of a drinking glass from the kitchen — *Tips For Brooke*. My younger brothers, barely old enough to decide what they wanted for lunch, were to act as ushers, making sure players moved from table to table, swiftly and efficiently. My old next-door neighbor, Ben, was to be the referee. He showed up five hours early with a whistle around his neck, his entire *Yu-Gi-Oh* card collection in a thick blue binder, and a double-sided red light saber attached to his belt loop in case things got out of hand. I was to be the grandmaster, not competing today, just pacing around, stopping by the tables to make sure everyone was having a good time, shaking hands with the top players, smiling, nodding, excusing myself and going on my way, very much like my father at a family dinner party with lots of men in ties holding glasses of scotch; he would make his rounds, shake hands, everyone praising him for his beautiful house, his wonderful family, and his great Success.

We waited by the window — me, Brooke, Thomas, Donald, and Ben. We'd passed out at least a hundred fliers at the local bookstore where every Saturday they held little *Yu-Gi-Oh* tournaments, kids dueling on the floor, parents stepping over the cards trying to peruse the books in the aisles — it was pathetic. No, us kids deserved something better. We deserved tables! We

53

deserved prizes! And if no one else was going to step up, well then who better than me?

Noses pressed to the window, we waited. Any minute now, the parade would arrive. We were anticipating hundreds of kids. The whole thing might even spiral out of control and I would need to call in more friends to referee, maybe even employ my parents, pull them aside, give them a quick rundown on the basics of *Yu-Gi-Oh*, explain the importance of professionalism, check their outfits, lead them downstairs to the arena and tell them, respectfully, knowing well how best to manage my subordinates, that I'd be watching their every move.

This was my tournament. Everything had to be perfect.

All of a sudden, a minivan pulled into the driveway. We bolted to the garage, welcoming who knows how many, five, ten, fifty kids!

We waited for the garage door to rise—*come on, come on*—and then barreled into the driveway, all of us shouting, "WELCOME TO THE FIRST EVER COLE'S NATIONAL *YU-GI-OH* TOURNAMENT!"

One kid. A seven year old, stepped out of the car with his mother. She was holding my flier. She said, "Is this the card game place?"

"It sure is!" I said, stepping forward.

"What time should I come back and pick him up?"

The kid picked his nose.

"We should be done by about four," I said, chin high. I was very mature for my age.

She turned her son over and drove away.

I made the kid go through the whole process. He followed the signs into the basement. My sister ran ahead of us to take her post at the cash register. "Five dollars, please!" and then eyed the tip jar as if this kid had another buck stashed in his pocket. We led him to the big tournament table, and he took a seat opposite of my brother, Thomas. Ben stood at the middle of the table to referee. They would duel until more players arrived.

Nobody else showed up. For three hours, we babysat this kid, wondering where we'd gone wrong, why this hadn't been a hit, why local news stations weren't holding lights up to my face and asking how someone so young had such an innate sense for entrepreneurship.

When all was said and done, and the kid left, and so did Ben, and my siblings were sufficiently disgruntled because none of them had made a cent, I took a seat at the kitchen table to reflect on my business plan. My dad, now sitting down with his afternoon cup of coffee, said, "And that's why you want to do well in school, Cole. Get a good job. Something that's already established. It's not so easy when you try to build it yourself, now is it?"

[Hot Doctor]: "Is it hard to focus in school, Cole?"

[Hot Doctor]: "Do you have trouble finishing your tests?"

[Hot Doctor]: "Why do you think your mother brought you here today?"

"Because she's wrong," I said.

My mother gave me the look. I was not cooperating.

[Hot Doctor]: "So you don't think you have ADD?"

"No, I don't have ADD."

[Hot Doctor]: "Do you know what ADD is?"

"I know I don't have it."

[Hot Doctor]: "Sometimes, ADD can come in different forms."

"Neat."

55

[Mom]: "Cole…"

[Hot Doctor]: "Why don't you think you have ADD?"

Because from the moment I logged into the World of Warcraft, to the moment I logged off, I was focused. I was disciplined. I didn't think about school or upcoming exams or my parents or my teachers or how the girls in my classes would wear these short white skirts and for the whole class they'd have their legs crossed, like guards in front of castle doors, and I'd wait, wait for that unicorn moment when they would adjust and switch their legs — left over right instead of right over left — and for the briefest of moments I would see the light at the end of the tunnel, the bright yellow underwear hiding between their thighs.

When I was in the World of Warcraft, I forgot about all of that. And do you know why?

"Because I can focus on things I care about just fine."

[Mom]: "Well that's the problem, Cole. You have to be able to focus on the things you don't care about too."

"That's so stupid. Why do I have to spend time learning all this stuff that I'm never going to use?"

[Hot Doctor]: "Why don't we just do the test?"

[Mom]: "Yes, let's do the test."

"Great, let's test the kid who has VERY CLEARLY STATED THAT HE DOES NOT NEED TO BE TESTED."

The doctor lady walked to the corner of the room and pulled out the chair in front of an old computer.

[Hot Doctor]: "Now, I want you to look at this screen, and every time a little green dot appears, hit the spacebar."

I dragged myself over and took a seat. The screen was completely black, and the green dot she was referring to was the size of a toothpick tip.

"That's it?"

[Hot Doctor]: "That's it."

"Easy. How long do I do this for?"

[Hot Doctor]: "Forty-five minutes."

I howled like a howler monkey.

"WHAT?"

[Mom]: "Cole, stop complaining and just do it."

"Hold on. You want me to sit here and stare at a blank screen, looking for a tiny green dot, for forty-five minutes, and *that's* how you're going to determine whether or not I need medication?"

I seemed to be the only one in the room blown away by this asinine method of testing.

Neither of them responded.

"I want *YOU* to do this for forty-five minutes, and I bet it'll say that *YOU* have ADD *too!*"

[Hot Doctor]: "I'm starting the test. Are you ready?"

It was hopeless. They made me take it. And sure enough, within a matter of minutes, I was bored and had missed at least seven green dots, probably thirteen. I was doomed to fail.

Two weeks later, my fate was sealed. The doctor lady called home and instructed my dad to head to the pharmacy to pick up my prescription. My parents sat the whole family down in the living room and shared the news. I had a disorder.

I have ADD.

Chapter 4
Page Avenue

A little over a year into my journey inside the game, I made my first real friend on the Internet.

His name was Ez, and he was an Undead Priest. Ez was an incredible player, and I knew of him from the Wildhammer forums. He would troll other players to the point of glorious, raging embarrassment. He was witty, he was intelligent, and he was in the top Horde guild on the server, <Hording School>.

We met by chance in the decrepit fields of Sorrow Hill. A group of Alliance jumped me, and he swooped in at the last second to save the day. We ended up defeating them 2v5. Impressed by how well we played together, he messaged me saying he had a group running Warsong Gulch for Honor points and asked if I wanted to join. Since I had just hit Level 60 and started the Honor grind myself, I said sure.

The Honor system was a ruthless and competitive way to earn rewards in the World of Warcraft — a sort of alternative to raiding. There were 14 ranks, and you were awarded Honor points for defeating enemy Alliance players and winning Battlegrounds. Based on how many Honor points you accumulated throughout the week, come Tuesday, you would either rise or fall in rank. The lower ranks, Scout, Grunt, Sargent, awarded you nominal items such as a tabard to wear or a new cloak. The highest ranks, General, Warlord, High Warlord, unlocked items and weapons that glowed orange (or for the Alliance, glowed blue) and were idolized by every player in the game.

How the Honor system worked was similar to a grading curve. Your progress up the ladder each week was not determined just by your individual performance, but your performance in comparison to every other player on the server.

For example: Let's say you take a test and you get 18/20 questions correct. That's pretty good! You deserve a B! Right? Wrong. The Honor system would say, while you did in fact score an 18/20, that does not mean you will be receiving a B, because Johnny scored a 19/20 and Margarita scored a 20/20 and Ming Ling got all the extra credit right so he got a 30/20, meaning that although 18/20 was a good score, it actually wasn't all that great compared to everyone else, making your score less valuable.

Now let's say the following week, you score an 18/20 again. And let's even say that Johnny scored a 17/20 and Margarita didn't study so she scored a 14/20, and Ming Ling didn't get much sleep the night before because he was up practicing for his cello recital so he only got half the extra credit and ended up with a 25/20. You'd think, hey, maybe an 18/20 is pretty good now! But no, you'd be wrong again. Because over time (second week now), since you had climbed higher on the Honor system, the bar for which you were aiming was linearly raised. Meaning that while the 18/20 you received last week progressed you halfway to your next rank, the 18/20 you received this week only progressed you 40%.

The higher you climbed, the higher the expectation, and the more Honor you were required to earn in order to progress.

With this sliding algorithm in place, some servers decided, as a collective, that they would manipulate the system to provide more rewards for less effort. If Honor points were relative, they would simply lower the ceiling. Like a league of nations, guild leaders came together, decided on an Honor cap, and then demanded their members adhere — meaning that if the test was out of 20 questions and all the top guild leaders decided to cap the answers at 5, then getting a 5/20 was essentially the same thing as getting a 20/20 because nobody surpassed the cap, thus using a system based on relativity to their advantage. Less work, more rewards for everyone.

Wildhammer did the complete opposite.

Instead of working together, Wildhammer's top guilds and most dedicated players bled the Honor system so dry that only the totally insane, the sleep deprived and caffeine addicted, the test takers that could score 100/20 were able to succeed. Where other servers set caps at 60,000 Honor points per week, the Wildhammer community pushed the cap to about 500,000.

In order to keep up, players were often forced to share accounts, meaning that while the original owner slept or went to work, someone else took a shift and played that person's character to keep the Honor points rolling in. Sometimes, there were as many as five people on one account, alternating throughout the day to ensure the character's success. This, of course, was risky business. The worst happened to a Dwarf Rogue on Wildhammer named Thaeds, whose account information fell into the wrong hands. Someone took his Rogue into Orgrimmar and killed computer-generated civilians for about four hours. Killing civilians was the opposite of an Honor kill, and reduced your Honor rank. The next day, the day Thaeds was expecting to hit Rank 14, he logged online and found his Rogue sitting naked in Stormwind, back at Rank 1. Rumor had it that he fell into a dark depression and vanished from the World of Warcraft for almost two months, only to return a completely different person, adamantly against any sort of competitive play that could possibly lead him back down the twisted path from whence he came. The Honor grind was no joke.

On the forums, retired Rank 14's warned the young and ambitious. They shared Before and After pictures of them in real life — Before The Grind: Thumbs up in front of their computer, smiling, innocence in their eyes. After The Grind: Defeated, malnourished, a sadness in their drooping face. They said it wasn't worth it. Go spend time with your friends. Enjoy the game. Don't let the Honor system kidnap your soul.

Did I listen? Of course not! I would watch PvP videos online made by Rank 14 Undead Mages, the Rank 14 staff resting on their backs, a stream of red magic flowing behind them, their black, spiky shoulders glowing orange; and the way it made them look, my God, it was power I'd never seen. It demanded respect. It laughed in the face of fear. It was the highest form of Success a player could reach, and it was right there on my computer screen. It was accessible to me! Me! A fifteen-year-old kid! I wouldn't have to endure years of organized education to earn wealth or prestige I wouldn't have to go to med school or get straight A's. Rank 14 would prove that World of Warcraft was a worthwhile endeavor, and that I possessed the very same traits that had crafted the great leaders of our world.

This is how my friendship with Ez began, both of us pledging our allegiance to the Honor grind.

There was just one problem.

By now, my parents had become less than tolerant of my time in front of the computer. We were at war with each other, and I was constantly defending my right as an adolescent to unwind after eight hours spent at school. They allowed me thirty minutes a day. That's it. If I wanted to play World of Warcraft any longer than that, I would need to earn the right by bringing home straight A's, or play the game without them knowing.

Obviously I became a very sneaky child.

Every night, when 10:00 p.m. struck the clocks in our kingdom, my mother and father would patrol the house. Preemptively, I'd crawl into my bed and tuck myself in, sweet as an angel. I would pull the covers up to my chin and hug my knees close to my chest, and by the time my mother would peek her head into my room and say, "Cole?" I would already be fluttering my eyes and falling into a slumberous abyss.

With the moon pouring through the window and shining on her smiling face, she would whisper, "I love you. Goodnight!"

And right back, in my last fading breath, I would exhale the important syllables of the echoing phrase, "Goodnihhh mahhh."

My heavy wooden door would be pulled closed, and at the very moment the golden handle fastened itself into place, my eyes would burst open and begin counting down the minutes on my red digital clock.

At exactly 10:15 p.m., I would begin my nightly ritual. I would carefully peel the covers off my body and fold them to the side, climbing out of bed. My naked feet would touch down on the carpet, and I would tiptoe to my door, my heavy wooden door. My parents had ears like Alcatraz spotlights. I could not make a sound. I would grab the golden doorknob with my right hand and press the door's edge with my left. I would push the door into the frame and turn the handle slowly, and when the knob was turned all the way, I would pull the door open, not a peep from the hinge.

I would peek my head out of the doorframe and look down the long hallway toward their master bedroom. I had been studying their routine for a while now. If their door was open, it meant they were still awake and I needed to retreat immediately. I would fall back into my room, turn the doorknob all the way to the left again, as not to catch the hinge, then slowly press the heavy wooden door back into its frame, only then releasing the handle.

If their door was closed but there was a thin light underneath, it meant they were almost ready to go to sleep, probably in bed talking, reading maybe, but the coast wasn't yet clear. No chances could be taken.

Sometimes, I would repeat this process three, seven, eleven times, checking the hallway, then crawling back into bed, the clock striking 11:00 p.m., 11:15 p.m., 11:30 p.m.

When I would finally gaze down the hallway and see their door was closed with no light underneath, even still, I would tiptoe forward a few feet, inching my way toward their fort, raising my ear to the air. I would listen for faint whispers, suspicious rustling, any sign that might warn me of a sudden ambush — my parents appearing in my doorway with the glow of my computer screen illuminating my face, catching me red handed.

If there were no whispers, no indications that they would soon wake and walk down the hallway, then and only then would I gently press my door closed and return to the World of Warcraft.

In my room's blackness, the only light coming from the moon sitting on my floor, I would sit tall in my computer chair and fasten my headset over my head. This was my most intimate action. No one could distract me at this hour. There was no pressing assignment, no plate left unwashed, no chore unattended to, no piano piece I should have been practicing. This was my time and my time only to develop myself as I saw fit.

Ez and his friends, Maull and Clitauren would already be online. They understood my situation, and knew why I couldn't log on until late at night. Sometimes, they had to perform similar rituals within their homes. We were all high school students navigating our parents' rules and expectations.

As soon as we started the Honor grind together, I became one of the guys. Ez, Maull, and Clitauren all went to the same school in Texas, and were on the hockey team together. They were best friends, and always called each other by their real names: Ez was Marve, Maull was Sam, and Clitauren was Landon.

And you'd think Marve was maybe the same as me: awkward, shy, hiding on the Internet. But he wasn't. Not him, not Sam, and not Landon. Marve was this six foot two Italian kid, and the captain of his hockey team. He was also one of the most hardcore World of Warcraft players I'd ever met. Hanging with them, I felt like I'd been invited to sit at the popular lunch table.

"We came back to my place, and I told her I wanted to stick it in her butt, and she said only if she got to stick a zucchini in mine first so I would know what it felt like," said Marve. I could tell he'd been drinking Red Bull again. He was way too energetic for how late it was.

"You could offer me a million dollars and I would never stick something that large up my anus," said Landon.

"Are you implying that you would stick something of moderate size up your anus?" said Marve.

"Landon, I've seen you eat 27 packets of hot sauce for five dollars. Pretty sure you'd stick a vegetable up your ass for the right price," said Sam.

"Fine. Twenty dollars and I might do it."

"I think what's most important here is figuring out where I can buy the world's smallest zucchini," said Marve, "because I really want to put it in her butt."

"What's up guys!" I said, half-whispering.

"Cole!" said Marve.

"What's up, Cole," said Sam.

"We're about to queue for another Battleground, you in?" asked Landon.

"Yup. Invite me."

A party invite appeared on my screen and we queued up for Warsong Gulch. It was 11:29 p.m. on a school night.

"Ok, so Sam, I have to tell you this. Today I got a call from Jess, right?" said Marve.

"Right."

"And she's sobbing. Like, sobbing dude. Sobbing to the point where I couldn't even understand what the fuck she was saying. And I'm trying to be the good boyfriend, you know, *what's wrong, what's wrong,* but she's just sobbing and sobbing and…"

"I get it. She's sobbing."

"Landon, just wait. It gets so good man," said Sam.

Our Warsong Gulch game began, and I followed Ez, Maull, and Clitauren out into the battlefield.

"So finally, I get her to calm down. I say, *babe, what is it?* And I told you how she was pregnant a couple weeks ago, right?"

My eyes widened and my mouth opened to ask, "I'm sorry, *what,*" because I had no idea kids our age were even having sex yet. I thought we were still on handjobs and blowjobs, which even that was a stretch since I'd yet to experience either. But I didn't say a word. I didn't want to give away my lack of knowledge in this area when they seemed to be so well educated. But also because right now, our four-man militia was taking on an entire ten-man army of Alliance, and my brain couldn't really ask that question and Sheep the Priest and Counterspell the Paladin and kill the Rogue all at the same time.

They, on the other hand, had no problem multi-tasking.

"You're a fucking idiot, Marve," said Landon.

"Dude…"

"I know, I know. *The condom broke.*"

"IT'S NOT MY FAULT!"

On my screen, one by one, every Alliance player fell to the ground. Ez, Maull, and Clitauren seemed unfazed. They were some of the best players I'd ever played with.

"Whatever. Just tell your goddamn story," said Landon.

"So, Cole, to catch you up here," said Marve, "I got my girlfriend pregnant a couple weeks back."

I tried, best I could, to respond in their same sort of banter, but it was intimidating. These guys were not your typical Internet nerds. They had smoking hot girlfriends — Marve, wanting to be funny, had sent me pictures that proved it: this blonde girl who, in all honesty, could have been a porn star, big boobs popping out of her skin tight halter top, holding up a sign that said, "I'm with Ez," with Marve giving the camera two thumbs up. He said he made her refer to him by his World of Warcraft name because he said it would train her to get used to the fact that she took second priority.

"You got her pregnant? That sucks," I said. The way I said

it sounded like I knew the struggle well — I got girls pregnant all the time.

"Yeah, it does. Well, it did..."

"DON'T RUIN IT, MARVE."

"JESUS, SAM, I'M NOT RUINING THE GODDAMN STORY."

Now I was laughing along with them.

"So anyways, Landon, as I was saying…"

"As you were saying…"

"Right, as I was saying. Jess calls me up while I'm in class. She usually never calls me during school, so I figured it must be important."

"Ok."

"Cole, Jess goes to another school," said Sam, keeping me informed.

"Got it."

"And when she finally calmed down, she goes, *Marve, I have to terrible news.* And I'm like, *babe, what is it, you can tell me.* And she goes…"

Knowing the punch line, Sam let out a wail of laughter so loud that his mic crackled and burst all of our eardrums.

"…She goes, *this morning, I had a miscarriage.*"

"No fucking way," said Landon.

Sam was laughing hysterically in the background.

And all of a sudden, I got really sad. Maybe it wasn't sadness, I don't know. It was a weird feeling. Sad, bothered, weird, just weird. I felt weird. My head said I should feel really, really sad, but my chest was more curious, having trouble believing that these things I'd heard about in movies — teenage sex, unplanned pregnancies, *miscarriages* — actually happened in real life. I was fifteen. What did I know about the world? Nothing. I knew nothing.

Right as I was about to step up to the plate, open my mouth and say something consoling, I would be the consoling one here, "Dude, I am so sorry…" Marve said first: "Yeah man, how incredible is that?"

"You might be the luckiest guy alive," said Landon.

"Dude, I know! I swear, I swear on mother Mary's vagina, the moment those words came out of her mouth, I felt like, if there is a God, he was staring down at me from heaven saying, *now Marve, promise you'll only have sex with girls on birth control.*"

"I've been saying that from the beginning," said Sam.

"Did she birth it in the toilet?" asked Landon.

"Shower."

"Christ. Probably looked like a murder scene in there."

"Sure as hell hope so," said Marve. "I want that baby *gone.* I'm not ready to be a father."

"No shit," said Landon.

I tried to put himself in Marve's shoes. As fucked up as the whole situation was, I couldn't help but agree. If I was sixteen and had gotten my girlfriend pregnant, I could only imagine the ridicule that would accompany an abortion — I would never suggest she keep it. Sixteen? SIXTEEN? I couldn't be a father at sixteen. No, a quiet passing in the shower was best-case scenario.

"Marve, someone should make a law that says even when you're 33, you still can't become a father," said Landon.

"I would vote for that law," said Sam.

I was so focused on the conversation that I didn't even realize we'd won our Warsong Gulch game and were sitting in queue for another. It was 12:30 a.m. I had school in the morning. I knew I was going to be dead tired if I didn't go to sleep soon, but I didn't care. Hanging out in Ventrilo with Marve, Sam, and Landon, telling stories, laughing and joking around was the most fun I'd ever had playing World of Warcraft.

And then he said it. Marve said, quite possibly, the most revealing comment to ever grace the Internet.

"I'm just so happy, man. Thank God that baby is dead. Now I won't have to quit playing World of Warcraft."

That's when I realized just how far in we all were — because I'd been thinking the exact same thing. Becoming a father would mean getting a job, supporting a family, and inevitably, quitting the game.

"I was worried we'd have to find a new Priest," said Landon.

"Don't worry, I'd have sent a hitman for the child," said Sam.

I started to laugh. I don't know what was so funny. I shouldn't have been laughing. But I started laughing so hard I couldn't breathe. Then they started laughing. And we all couldn't stop. The truth is, we were just a bunch of teenagers, wandering through the world, happy to have found common ground.

This is what made the Honor grind tolerable. Our friendship.

What made the Honor grind exhausting were all the hours we had to endure playing Real Life.

Immediately after I was diagnosed with ADD, my parents quickly put me on medication.

[Dad]: "Time to build some new study habits!"

69

He came strolling over to the kitchen table with a glass of water in his right hand and a pink pill in his left. I had a Geometry test the next day. I hated Geometry. Every question was a test of my patience, asking me to, "Prove that this is a rectangle." Out of frustration, I often thought it best to retort, "Because my kindergarten teacher said so." Algebra, fine. Find X. I saw the relevance. Sometime in the future, I would be at the grocery store doing my own shopping, and I would want to know which of the two milk cartons — off-brand versus brand name — was cheaper based on fluid ounces per dollar. Mental algebra would save me twenty cents here, a few bucks there. But Geometry? When would I ever be at the grocery store comparing two bottles of maple syrup and come to the conclusion that, ah, you know what, I bet I would know which one is cheaper if I could prove that one bottle is in fact not a parallelogram.

[Dad]: "The dosage says to take one pill before you begin studying."

We were about to try out my new medication. It was 6:00 p.m.

[Me]: "I bet it doesn't even do anything."

[Dad]: "We're about to find out."

I grabbed the pill from his hand and swallowed it with a sip of water. I knew what he was thinking. He was thrilled. He was waiting to see his son transform before his very eyes. I would take this little pink pill and be fixed. I wouldn't have to work at Jewel Osco after all. I would be like every other kid in this town — thank God. I would wake up early; I would stay after school; I would bolt for the cafeteria to see if I'd made the Math team. With this little pink pill, I would be cured of my negligence, my stupidity, my disobedience.

When it was down the hatch, I opened my mouth like an inmate at a mental hospital. My dad, skeptical, peered in at different angles. When all was clear, he gave me the nod and I closed my mouth.

70

As my dad set up at the kitchen table, I took this wonderful opportunity to play a trick on Brooke. I walked over to her in the living room, dead faced, and sat down next to her, still as a corpse.

[Brooke]: "What do you want, Cole."

I turned slowly toward her, all life from my eyes withdrawn.

[Me]: "Nothing. Just took my ADD medication."

With this deadened look on my face and a severe lack of knowledge on her part of what this medication would actually do to me, the thought that she'd lost her fun and energetic brother forever hit her, and she burst into tears.

[Brooke]: "NO! COLE!"

I kept my face still as stone.

[Me]: "It's ok. I'm better now."

No smile. Monotone.

[Brooke]: "DAD, WHAT DID YOU DO TO HIM..."

She was hysterical. My dad came into the room.

[Dad]: "Brooke, what's the matter?"

She pointed at me, and then punched my shoulder, trying to wake me up.

[Brooke]: "YOU PUT HIM ON THOSE STUPID PILLS."

I finished my brilliant performance by looking up at my father, without expression.

[Me]: "Looks like the medication is working.... I'm finally... Normal."

Brooke had tears streaming down her cheeks.

71

And then for the grand finale, I leapt up from the couch and shouted at Brooke, "HAH, GOT YA!" I laughed so hard. It was very funny.

[Brooke]: "COLE THAT WASN'T FUNNY."

[Dad]: "Cole, that was very inappropriate."

[Me]: "Oh, come on. These pills probably won't even do anything. I'm fine."

And I was right. For ten, fifteen, twenty minutes, nothing happened. My dad and I worked through my homework at the kitchen table. Geometry was still boring. All I wanted to do was go back upstairs and continue playing World of Warcraft.

[Dad]: "Let's go over Chapter 8 again. You were having a lot of trouble with Chapter 8."

I rummaged through my folder for the Chapter 8 study guide. The folder was ripping apart. The pockets were stuffed with too many papers and all over the cover were tiny lists of homework from the days I'd forgotten my assignment notebook at home. My dad, who often suggested spiral binders, calendars, a filing cabinet in my bedroom, gave a little laugh —

[Dad]: "This is why we're putting you on the good stuff!"

All of a sudden, my head started to feel tight. Like someone had tied a hundred rubber bands around my forehead. The yellow pencil in my hand felt light. I looked at the yellow. It was pointed at the paper. On the paper was a trapezoid. I was supposed to do something with that trapezoid. I needed to write something down. I looked hard at the trapezoid.

[Dad]: "So, let's think through this first one. Based on the rules that you memorized, which ones would you use here to prove that this is a trapezoid?"

The rules. I knew them. Any second now I would start writing. I looked at the yellow pencil, and then the white, the paper.

Yellow, white. Pencil tip, trapezoid. My thoughts felt like massive boulders being thrown around as easily as ping pong balls — faster, faster. My eyes blinked like machine guns. I was biting my lip, *biting, biting,* bleeding inside my mouth.

[Dad]: "Still can't figure it out?"

Biting. Tapping. Yellow pencil, white paper, yellow white, yellow white. Knee bounce. Knee bounce. Heart, boom boom, *boom boom,* **boom boom.**

[Dad]: "Here."

He reached for my yellow pencil.

[Dad]: "Let me show you a little trick."

In one swift motion, I tilted my head to the ceiling, let out a wild scream, and slammed my face down onto the table, my Geometry textbook cushioning the fall. I started sobbing. I grabbed my hair and pulled. It felt like my brain was on fire.

[Dad]: "Cole? Cole what's wrong? Geometry isn't that bad."

My mom and sister came running in from the living room.

[Mom]: "Is everything alright?"

[Dad]: "I… I don't know what happened. We were having a great time studying, and all of a sudden…"

Brooke started crying again.

[Brooke]: "What's happening!"

I picked my head up and started yelling.

[Me]: "WHY DID YOU MAKE ME TAKE THAT STUPID PILL. MAKE IT STOP. MAKE IT STOP, PLEASE."

In a matter of minutes, I had gone from zero to out-of-control. My chest rattled like a Jeep off-roading in the mountains, and my eyes were wide as 8 balls. It felt like if I didn't take a syringe and start draining my brain, my head was going to explode. The world was moving a million miles a minute.

Brooke was crying into my mother's shoulder.

My parents conversed over the noise.

[Mom]: "Did you give him the right dosage?"

[Dad]: "It said to take one! I only gave him one!"

[Mom]: "Cole, we really need to know if this is real or if you're just exaggerating."

I stood up, my hands still clutching my hair, pulling it sideways.

[Me]: "DOES IT LOOK LIKE I'M EXAGGERATING, MOM?"

[Mom]: "Ok, ok."

She looked at my dad.

[Mom]: "The doctor did say it might take some experimenting to find the right medication..."

[Me]: "YEAH WELL CLEARLY THIS ONE ISN'T IT."

Convinced that this was just part of the process, my parents promptly excused me upstairs to go try and relax. They rang the doctor lady to request a different medication. She said not to worry, this happened all the time with Concerta — this very normal feeling as if the patient has just snorted fifty eight lines of cocaine — and called in a new prescription. The fact that self-induced mania was common in the world of pharmaceuticals was astonishing to me.

For the rest of the night I sat up in my bed, tapping my knees, waiting for the medication to wear off. I tried playing World of Warcraft after everyone went to bed, but it made me too anxious. I finally fell asleep around five in the morning.

74

I returned home from school the next day exhausted, a new pill bottle in my mother's hand.

[Mom]: "We picked this up for you."

She said it as if she'd gotten me a gift.

[Me]: "Great. Can't wait to have another heart attack."

[Mom]: "This one is different. It's a much lighter dose."

[Me]: "I would like to state for the record that in no way do I support this."

[Mom]: "Cole, you saw the test results. You need a little extra help."

Glass of water in my right hand, a white pill now in my left, I threw it back and swallowed. My mother smiled.

I went upstairs and took a seat at my desk. I suppressed the urge to turn toward my computer and log into the World of Warcraft. I had a quiz on Friday and really needed to study. Contrary to popular belief, I wasn't irresponsible. I knew it was in my best interest to maintain a somewhat respectable grade point average.

My plan was to study for an hour, maybe an hour and a half, and when my mother took Brooke to her violin lesson, I'd take my World of Warcraft break. That was the plan.

I ended up studying for seven hours straight. Seven. Hours. Non-stop. And when I did take a break, it wasn't really a break at all; it was an interruption, by my dad, who had come by to bring me a peanut butter and jelly sandwich (wheat).

He opened the door.

[Dad]: "How's the studying going, champ?"

My eyes were dilated and my mouth tasted like cotton and I couldn't get the words to come out fast enough.

[Me]: "Studying? Good. Going good. Dad. Look. Look at all my notes. Look."

I held up my notebook and started flipping pages. There were twenty, thirty, forty sheets of loose leaf, all written in perfect cursive, bullet points, charts, drawings immaculate to the point of art. I had no idea what any of it meant. But I was high on Ritalin, and for some reason it made perfect sense for me to copy, word for word, everything that was in my textbook into my notebook as neatly as humanly possible.

[Dad]: "Cole, this is incredible!"

[Me]: "Yeah. It's ok. Pretty good. Good stuff. I like it. I'm learning a lot. I just learned about atoms. And electrons. Lots of electrons. I think it was electrons. I did like twelve chapters. I only have a couple more. Maybe three. Seven, maybe. I can't remember. I need to keep studying. Did you need something?"

My dad left the peanut butter and jelly on my desk and quickly ran for the door.

[Dad]: "No, no. Keep up the good work. Don't let me distract you!"

I couldn't hear him. I was already back at it, my right wrist on fire from all the writing.

And then an hour or so later, I crashed. Face first, on my desk, out cold. My mom had to drag me from my desk chair into my bed.

In my parents' eyes, this second medication was a godsend, a gift from the holy land able to turn their uncooperative son into an obedient work mule. But when it came time for me to take my Chemistry test, I didn't perform any better. I recognized a few more vocabulary words, knew that I had seen this or that question somewhere before, but my grade remained the same — nothing more than average. The only thing Ritalin seemed to do was give me a headache the next morning. My brain was an engine that had been revved to death.

My parents, looking for grades they could be proud of, weren't very pleased with the return on their investment. They inquired with the doctor lady again as to why all this money was being spent on appointments and new medications that hadn't yet turned me into an Ivy League scholar. The doctor lady regurgitated her same script: "Amphetamines are a tricky beast. We have to find the right one for your son."

But despite my parents' and several doctors' recommendations, I refused further participation. I shut my lips tight and denied their efforts — and I wasn't the only kid. At school, in the mornings or during lunch, other kids would trade their medications with each other. I would listen to them talk about how some made you feel jittery, or calm, or "like speed." Some kids hated it, some loved it. But one thing was certain: there were plenty of drugs in our wealthy town to go around.

My parents didn't know what to do with me. They were loving. They cared so much. They weren't about to force-feed medications that obviously weren't working. But they had it in their minds that we were close, so close to finding a cure for my behavior.

Books started popping up all over the house: *Understanding ADD: A Parent's Perspective. ADD: Why It's Not Your Fault.* In a strange way, this ended up being the perfect distraction. My mother and father were so busy trying to figure out how to fix me that I was able to sneak back to my computer for an extra half hour here, 45 minutes there, while they retreated to their bedroom earlier than usual, sharing books, comparing notes, discussing what in the world was wrong with their firstborn son. "Why isn't he performing as well as the other kids? Why isn't our child normal?"

It was during these highly stressful few months that Marve, Sam, Landon and I were neck-deep in the Honor grind — along with thousands of other players all over the world, competing to climb the ranks.

By the second month of our journey, the lack of sleep

became our biggest obstacle.

I was constantly delirious. I would sit at dinner, paranoid. Somehow my parents knew. They knew I was staying up past my bedtime! Oh, the shame! How could they not know? My God, the lie I was living behind their backs! I would not have been punished in any normal way, no no. I would have been asked — forced! — to drag my computer out into the driveway, given a sledgehammer, and then ordered to destroy the thing into a million little pieces. I would have been sent away, in all seriousness, to a boarding school that specialized in castration. I would have been made to audition for Dr. Phil (and if there was no such thing as auditioning for Dr. Phil, then I would invent it; I would be the first). When given the opportunity to make an appearance on the show — I would of course make an appearance, my mother would see to that — I would go on to tell hundreds of thousands of emotional child-bearers everywhere, all over the world, that video games were, quite possibly, the most dangerous thing on this planet. Even more dangerous than cocaine, mostly because they're so accessible. It's as if cocaine is being sold to our children, right here in the malls, can you believe that? I said mothers, can you believe that! And they would shout back, "We can't believe it!" And I would raise my fist into the air and they'd bring out the big check, a donation, made out to Moms Of America, and I would shake Dr. Phil's hand, and together we would put an end to addiction, to violence, to video games!

The truly unhealthy exhaustion didn't quite settle in until about the third month, right around when most players gave up. My goal was to hit Rank 10, rewarding me with at least the first full set of armor. But the week I hit Rank 7, I started to realize the toll the grind was taking on my body. We could all feel it: Marve, Sam, Landon, and me. We only allowed ourselves four or five hours of sleep a night, and on weekends we would pull all-nighters, sleep through the morning, and then log back on at noon for a second shift, going all the way through the night again. Most of our late-night conversations sounded like this:

"I was in class yesterday and I realized I was daydreaming

about my bed," said Marve.

"I've done that," said Sam.

"My teacher was talking, and all I could think about were my pillows, and my blankets, and my teddy bears..." said Marve.

"Dude, stop. I'm so fucking tired. No talking about beds," said Landon.

It was 3:30 a.m. on a Wednesday.

"Guys, I just poured Red Bull into my bag of potato chips because I thought it was cereal," said Sam. "I might be losing my mind."

"This morning, I poured orange juice into my cereal and ate the whole thing without even noticing it wasn't milk," said Landon. "Then I laughed hysterically by myself at the table for ten minutes."

"Today at school, I got frustrated in the hallway because I couldn't Teleport ahead of people, and I kept thinking it was because my Blink was on cooldown," I said. Blink was a Mage ability. I wasn't joking.

"Damn, that's bad," said Sam.

"Yeah Cole, that's some mental ward shit," said Marve.

We all started crying laughing. Then ten minutes later, we were dead silent. Until one person started to doze off and someone would scream, "NO FALLING ASLEEP," and we'd all be manic and hysterical again.

I started taking naps in the nurse's office during lunch. I slept all through study hall. In class, I had to physically hold my eyelids open to stay awake, my pointer finger pushing up, thumb pulling down, stretching the skin on my face. I would dig my fingernails into my thighs, bite my lip until it bled, anything to keep from fading and being reprimanded by a teacher. Sometimes, I would come home from school and fake a stomachache just to get out of flashcards with Dad, or having to practice the piano, and I would leap into bed instead. I'd set my alarm for 11:00 p.m. and fall asleep in seconds. My pillows felt like clouds, my sheets the arms of angels...

...and then my alarm would sound in the deep of the night, and I'd begin the grind all over again.

The only reason any of us were able to endure the grueling process of the Honor grind was because of our friendships with each other. If Marve, Sam, Landon and I hadn't been trading stories, laughing together, helping each other stay awake, none of us would have made it. We were all suffering together — and that's what made it so special.

Since these guys were such well-known players on Wildhammer and friends with all the other top players, I started to meet other players through them. Even Alliance enemies they had befriended would come into our Ventrilo channel to trade stories while we all continued working toward our goals in the World of Warcraft.

And these weren't just kids like us. Some of them were, but they were also lawyers, single moms, fraternity presidents, software engineers. Through the World of Warcraft, I was introduced to people of all ages, denominations, and social statuses — and as a result, my view of the real world drastically began to broaden. I'd kill Alliance in Warsong Gulch while listening to a stockbroker explain the intricacies of Wall Street. I'd duel players in front of Orgrimmar while a 28-year-old cubicle slave warned of the slow torture that came with a corporate career. I got first-hand accounts of what life was like outside my protective bubble of rich white suburbia, and it was enthralling. So much so, that it slowly began to reshape how I saw my own peers — and subsequently, the town I was trapped within. I realized there was a much bigger world out there, and I was hungry for exploration.

One night, Marve, Sam, Landon and I were up late playing Battlegrounds, and one of our Alliance companions joined our Ventrilo channel. He was an older guy, this Alliance Paladin, and we'd seen him in a bunch of Warsong Gulch games. In our typical fashion, we posted on the forums and invited him to come hang out with us.

"So where you from?" Ez said.

"Hawaii, man."

"Hawaii? No fucking way."

"Yeah way."

"Is your computer out in the sand?"

We all laughed. These late night conversations were some of the best nights of my life.

"Pretty close. It's on the sun deck, but there's a screen around it so bugs and shit don't get in."

"That's fucking awesome."

"Can you hear the ocean behind me?"

We went silent, as if our ears were pressed close to a conch shell.

"I think I can hear it actually, yeah," said Marve.

"Shut the fuck up, you can't hear shit," said Landon.

While this was going on, we were in and out of Warsong Gulch and Arathi Basin, doing as we always did — grinding Battlegrounds for Honor points.

"What brought you to Hawaii?" asked Marve. "Or were you born there?"

"No, not born here. Came here with my wife, actually."

"Oh, nice. How long you guys been there?"

A strange silence entered the conversation.

"She's not here anymore, actually."

81

Never being one to accept such a vague answer, Marve continued.

"You divorced?"

The next time this older man, this Alliance Paladin spoke up, there was a numbness in his voice. Something wasn't right.

"Not exactly."

"Well spill man!" said Marve. "Tell us what happened!"

"Eh, I don't know," he said, like a bearded man at a bar, asked to tell a war story.

Sam and Landon egged him on.

"Come on!"

"Yeah, we're just grinding Honor bored as shit. Tell us the story."

Just then, our Warsong Gulch game ended, and our character's reappeared in the Horde main city of Orgrimmar.

"If you insist," he said.

"We do. We do insist," said Marve.

Thus began one of the most memorable nights I'd ever spent in the World of Warcraft.

"My wife and I moved to Hawaii a couple years ago. We came down here for vacation and ended up staying. I got a job doing finance, nothing fancy, but more than enough to live on here in paradise."

We all chuckled in agreement. Who wouldn't want to live in Hawaii?

"And you know, things were great, she got pregnant, we were thrilled for our first kid…"

Marve interrupted.

"That's great man, congrats!"

"Yeah, congrats," said Sam.

The man didn't respond. Just let the words hang in the air, and then continued on with his story.

"But there were some complications with the birth. Well, not exactly with the birth, more right after the birth."

"What do you mean?" said Marve.

"Do you guys know what post-partum depression is?"

This Paladin was a man. We were just kids.

"I've heard about it," said Marve.

"Yeah, they mentioned it in Health class. But what is it?" said Sam.

I didn't know either.

"It's where the mother goes through severe depression after she has the child."

"Oh yeah, now I remember," said Marve.

"Well, that's what happened. They put her on all this medication, tried to turn things around, but she just wasn't the same. She lost her mind."

All of our characters were standing still in Orgrimmar, our ears on high alert, listening so intently to this man tell his story that we were unable to play World of Warcraft at the same time. Here was a guy none of us had ever met before, sharing intimate details about his life. It was as if we'd known each other for years.

"So what happened," said Marve.

The man didn't sound like he was about to cry. What he

sounded like was that he'd cried for too many years, and couldn't cry any more.

"Well," he said, and in the pause that followed, we all inched to the edge of our desk chairs. Despite us all living in different parts of the country, in this moment, over the Internet, we were together.

"One day, I came home from work, and I saw her car in the driveway. Which was odd, because usually she took Sky, that was our daughter's name, Sky, usually she took Sky to the beach. I saw her car, walked inside, and started calling her name."

In my mind, the scene began to unfold. The man walking through the front door... The ocean's breeze passing through the open windows... The hardwood floors, sandy with his wife's footprints...

"I walked through the kitchen, the den, nowhere. I couldn't find her."

It was like watching a movie.

"And then I walked into the family room..."

We all held our breath.

"...and there she was, on the floor, with Sky, laying in her own blood. She had killed herself, and taken Sky with her."

All at once, as if we too had walked into that family room and seen the dead bodies, we said, "*No way.*"

"Dude, WHAT," said Marve.

"You can't be serious," said Sam.

"Look it up if you don't believe me," he said.

This was the Internet after all. Anyone could say anything.

[Party][Ez]: Hop on AIM. I'm gonna see if this dude is forreal.

[Party][Cackle]: Ok, be right there.

[Party][Ez]: This shit is too fucking nuts.

It was true. All of it. The guy gave Marve his town and real name and sure enough, he found the news article online: *Local Mother and Daughter, Lost to Suicide.*

This man had opened his heart and revealed something about his life none of us would have known otherwise. This was my first real exposure to some of the heartache that existed in the real world.

"I'm so sorry," said Marve.

"I don't know what to say," said Sam.

"Yeah, that's really intense," said Landon.

"Yeah," I said. That's all. It was too much. I didn't want to say the wrong thing.

"So, I have to ask," said Marve, after the initial shock had worn off. "What is a guy like you doing hanging out with a bunch of nerds in the World of Warcraft?"

The man let out a little laugh.

"Hawaii might be beautiful, but there's a lot of pain here too." His voice was low and dusty, as if that one wound had aged him a hundred years. He was only 29. "Not much money. Mediocre jobs. A lot of guys here, they give up on life, go to the one bar in town and drink themselves to death. I figure, I could either do that, or I could get myself some epic armor and fight for something."

It was so profound. And it opened the door for the rest of us.

Marve said, "I know what you mean. A lot of guys at my school think I'm this asshole that likes to get fucked up and get into fights, and girls think I'm a manwhore that'll fuck anything with legs..."

"Because you will," said Sam.

"Only sometimes!" said Marve.

We laughed.

"But seriously. Nobody knows why I do all this crazy shit, why I get myself thrown out of class, or why I sleep with these psycho sluts from my school, and I never really thought about it before, but I guess I do it because I don't want people to see that I actually have a heart and shit. I actually really care about people, and deep down I'm just a huge nerd. I'd much rather play video games. I guess that's why I love World of Warcraft. Because I feel like on the Internet I can actually be myself."

"Sounds like a good reason to play to me," said the man.

Hours passed like this, going around the circle, sharing things we'd never told anyone else, maybe never even admitted to ourselves.

By the time it was my turn, the sun was just coming up. We were all still wide awake.

"What about you, Cackle? I'm sure there's a reason why World of Warcraft means so much to you," the man said.

All this time, I'd been listening to everyone else, not really thinking about my own reasons for playing.

"Well," I said. Any minute now, my dad would be awake, walking downstairs for his Saturday morning cup of coffee.

Despite my wanting so badly to be seen as something similar — cool, confident, popular — I couldn't help but be honest. They had all been honest with me. I wanted to be honest with them.

"I think I play World of Warcraft because... Because I'm afraid to be myself in Real Life. I don't really know how to make friends at my school."

It felt so strange coming from my own mouth. I'd thought

the words a million times in my head, but to actually feel them on my tongue, see them out in front of me, dug up a completely different feeling. And they didn't laugh. They didn't make fun of me. They just hummed in acknowledgment.

"You seem like a good kid. What makes you think you can't be yourself?" asked the Paladin.

I thought about it.

"Honestly, I don't know. I'm just not interested in doing what other kids do, getting drunk, chasing girls. And I feel like you sort of have to be like that if you want people to like you. But I'd rather set goals and achieve them."

"Can I tell you something, Cackle?" said the man. "Years from now, when high school is over, and you and all your peers are out in the real world, they're going to be exactly the same. They're going to be getting drunk, chasing girls. They're never going to grow up. Meanwhile, you'll be setting goals and achieving them."

All by myself in my bedroom, the sun began to rise. I smiled.

"And besides," said Marve. "We're your friends."

Chapter 5
Make Them Hear You

After four hours of sleep, I was right back at my computer.

I could hear my mother down the hallway with two of her friends. She was giving them a tour of the house. Always a tour of the house.

[Mom]: "And here is Brooke's room. We had the curtains shipped from a specialty shop in Vancouver. It took months for them to arrive but I think it was worth the wait, don't you?"

[Mrs. Baker]: "Oh my gosh, absolutely. They're darling."

[Mrs. Monahan]: "And they match the bedspread perfectly!"

[Mom]: "I was going for this warm vintage motif, a little blend between gold and white, not too creamy but I didn't want sleek and shiny either."

Moments later, there was a knock at my door.

[Mom]: "Cole?"

Three heads peeked into my private domain. I quickly alt-tabbed out of the World of Warcraft to a Wikipedia page of Abraham Lincoln I had open in my browser, and changed the punk rock blaring from my computer speakers to a tear-jerking ballad sung by an African American acappella group called *Three Mo Tenors*. My mom loved this group. She'd given me their CD. And with Mr. Lincoln's firm portrait on my screen and rich, classical voices ringing from my computer speakers, it gave the sudden appearance that I was a cultured and distinguished young man, educating my eyes and ears on a Saturday afternoon.

The operatic song was called *Make Them Hear You.*

I spun toward the door in my computer chair and greeted the middle-aged women with a warm welcome.

[Cole]: "Hey Mom. Hello Mrs. Baker, Mrs. Monahan. How are you doing today?"

The two mothers muttered out something of a collective response, too awestruck by my manners to respond coherently. My mother and I moved along with the scene.

[Mom]: "Are we bothering you?"

[Cole]: "Me? No, no, you're not bothering me. Never bothering me!"

Meanwhile:

[Party][Ez]: CACKLE WHERE ARE YOU

[Party][Maull]: God dammit, he must be AFK

[Party][Clitauren]: God fucking dammit Cackle I'm too tired for this shit.

[Party][Ez]: Relax Landon, I'm sure he had a good reason

[Party][Maull]: CAAAAAAACKLEEEEEEEEE COME BACKKKKKK

[Party][Clitauren]: Fuck this, if he's AFK then I'm gonna go make some popcorn and jerk off

[Party][Maull]: That's an erotic combination.

[Mom]: "I just wanted to show them your new bookshelves!"

Ah yes, the bookshelves. Not me, no. This had nothing to do with me. This was about the bookshelves! The ones that leaned at an angle, charcoal black, very chic.

[Mom]: "Speaking of books, Cole just gave a really great presentation in his English class on *Wuthering Heights*. Do you remember reading that back in high school? I sure do."

[Mrs. Monahan]: "It's been years since I read it, but I do remember."

[Mrs. Baker]: "How did the presentation go, Cole?"

I sat up tall in my chair. Chin, lifted. Smile, delightful.

[Cole]: "Oh, it went great! I spent a lot of time preparing, which I think really helped."

What I'd really done was procrastinate until the night before, skimmed over the first page, learned that the main character's name was Heathcliff, and then improvised my entire presentation: "You know what was so interesting about Heathcliff was that he, being the main character, really went through a lot of changes. I mean a lot of changes. He started off as, well, how most main characters start off, full of opportunity, and that's what the author does so well is take the main character, Heathcliff, through a personal journey, where by the end of the novel I mean wow, just wow, Heathcliff is a completely different person! And yet, at the core, still so much the same. And that's what makes *Wuthering Heights* such a classic, at least to me, because that's something we can all relate to, you know? That feeling of changing entirely, and yet at the same time, not really changing at all."

My mom turned toward her two friends, very animated now.

[Mom]: "Cole is having a pretty incredible Sophomore year, aren't you Cole?"

[Cole]: "Honestly? Really great. Maybe the best year ever."

Actually, I sort of wanted to kill myself. Turnabout was coming up and all these girls were doing such cool things, really cool things for the guys they were asking — making posters, interrupting class periods while singing off-key, "Will you go to Turnabout with me?" One girl even got the Vice Principal to say at the end of the morning announcements, "And one last thing: Mike Pritsker, Jamie Courrig wants to know if you'll go to Turnabout with her." Mike was in my class. Everyone started cheering and clapping and I sat there in the back row, hands in my pockets, knowing pretty much for certain that all four years of high school were going to go by and I was never going to know the feeling of my name being read over the intercom with a girl asking me to Turnabout too.

[Mom]: "Cole had to stop playing hockey this year because he fractured his spine. But we think it happened for a reason. Right, Cole?"

[Cole]: "Right."

I agreed with her so we could move this conversation along. I needed to get back to the World of Warcraft.

[Mom]: "Now Cole has more time to focus on the arts! He's learning this new Beethoven piece on the piano and really loving it."

[Cole]: "Oh, absolutely. Great piece. Lots of fun chords."

I enjoyed bagging rotten grass clippings more than I enjoyed practicing that piece.

[Mom]: "Do you think you could come downstairs and play a little for them? I'm sure they'd love to hear."

[Mrs. Baker]: "Yes, yes!"

[Mrs. Monahan]: "That would be wonderful!"

I threw my hand forward, *oh ladies.*

[Cole]: "I would love to, really I would, but Mom, I'm still struggling with the second movement, you know where it transitions to a major, happier feel? I'd rather get it perfect first and then play for an audience."

I smiled at them. I despised playing for guests.

[Mom]: "Completely understand, honey. Why don't you and I practice the transition later together?"

She turned to her friends.

[Mom]: "He loves music. As a baby, I would carry him around the living room and we'd dance. It was the only way to get him to stop crying. But it had to be either French opera at full volume or Celine Dion. Anything else and he'd throw a fit."

[Cole]: "Mom!"

[Mom]: "It's true!"

[Cole]: "Yeah but you don't have to tell *them* that!"

She laughed, *ha ha.*

I laughed, *ha ha.*

Do you see what kind of picture I'm painting here?

My parents would give these tours of the house, friends of theirs parking their cars under our basketball hoop, walking up the brick circle drive, entering our world — friends that often came from suburbs lesser than ours, careers that didn't quite pay what a spine surgeon makes. Lovely friends though, and sometimes they brought their kids. And if their kids were around my age then I was expected to entertain them while my mother and father took the adults through every wing, up every banister, down every hallway — "The original owner of the house was Dick Portillo, you know, Portillo's Hot Dogs? You should have seen the paint job, weiner dogs all over the walls. It was adorable, but it had to go. It just didn't match what we were trying to do with the carpet."

The kids would follow me up to my room. I'd open the

door and they'd say, "Wow." I'd offer them things: we could play Xbox, Dreamcast, we could watch a movie, but they'd just pace around and keep saying, "Wow," until eventually finding the courage to finish their thought aloud. "Your room is like, the size of my basement," and I'd just keep offering them things because I felt like I had so much, maybe if I offered them enough, showed how none of this mattered to me, not the new dresser or the two thousand dollar desk or the autographed Michael Jordan jersey framed and hung above my bed, they would see me as an equal instead of a child drowning in privilege. But they never did.

It was so hard for me to explain. I didn't pick the size of my room. I didn't ask for the armoire in the corner or the king-size bed. A regular bed would have done just fine. Actually, I would have been satisfied with a sleeping bag and a couple pillows; I didn't need much, I swear. But everything was picked out for me. The pictures on my walls were my mother's choice. Same with the clothes and the dressers and the bookshelves. All for the tours, ugh, the tours. Look at our pool, look at our garden, look at the new BMW. My parents' friends would say things, so subtle they thought, but their words stained the hallways of our mansion: "Looks like you'll be able to go to whatever college you want, huh Cole — since Dad can foot the bill." And I'd have to nod, smile, try to pretend like I wasn't hyperaware of my overwhelming position in society, knowing, even as young as ten, that their own children had less and would spend their whole lives reaching for the very things I took for granted.

It wasn't my parents' fault. It's not like they were self-centered, materialistic sheep that found purpose in this boasting. If anything, they *deserved* the tours — more tours, Mom and Dad, show it all! My parents had earned the right to bask in their success. We had nine bathrooms; their adolescent homes had had one. We had a pool with a waterfall Jacuzzi; they'd grown up with a birdbath in the backyard. They were living the American dream! No, it wasn't the tours I was upset about, because I knew that when I got older and inevitably became as successful as my father, I would probably be in the backyard, same as him, showing my buddies my new triple-story grill, pointing at my kids in the pool jumping from the Jacuzzi into the deep end, yelling for them to stop horsing around — "Hey, stop horsing around!" No, the tours I could live with. It was the way I got lumped in with them, paraded and positioned at the forefront of the family, viewed through a lens of measurable worth.

That's what made it so difficult. Every guest that walked the halls of our home was an audience member, and it was our task, not just as individuals, but pieces of the whole, to effectively market ourselves as a family — the perfect family. It was our job to shift the lens, not much, not to the point of removing all the things that made our family wonderful, only slightly; just enough to create a blind spot. And when these guests of ours would tour the halls and examine the walls, they would look at me with the same inquisition they would the painting of Florence hanging in our dining room. It made me feel like I was the same as the bookshelf, the king-size bed, the armoire. I was the handbag that hung from my mother's arm, the briefcase my father carried and placed in the passenger seat of his brand new BMW. I was an object, sculpted and tailored to fit the family image.

It made me feel like who I was already wasn't good enough.

My mother, standing in the doorway still, lifted her ear to my speakers, recognizing the song.

[Mom]: "Is this Three Mo' Tenors?"

[Me]: "Sure is."

[Mrs. Collins]: "Saturday afternoon, listening to opera?"

[Me]: "It's not quite opera, but it's close. My mom introduced me to it."

Mrs. Baker turned to my mom, an aching desperation to sculpt her own son welling in her eyes.

[Mrs. Baker]: "You have to tell me your secret."

95

And seriously, from the bottom of my heart, I would have performed all day for my mother, my father, for their friends and bosses and coworkers, and our extended family, and anyone that wanted to see the effects such a rich upbringing can have on the malleable mind of a child. I would have shown them the beautiful Beethoven that lingered on each one of my fingers. I would have stood at the front door, collected coats, shown our guests to the family room and handed them pamphlets detailing tonight's entertainment — "Tonight, you'll be listening to my sister Brooke on the violin, playing a very warm and delightful Minuet in G." I would have paraded my tongue of manners and modeled my newest wardrobe and embodied with full integrity an overwhelming thankfulness for my parents and all that they'd given me, had they allowed me one thing, just one thing, one thing was all I asked for.

The freedom to be me! As a fifteen-year-old journeying through life, what was most important was whatever had caught my interest. And right now, I was on my way to mastering the World of Warcraft. One day, I might even become a game designer, go to school for it, create a world even better than this one! But the fact that I couldn't share my ambition, couldn't be proud of what I loved, no different than how my mother was proud of her music, my father was proud of his medical practice, Brooke was proud of her violin, Thomas was proud of gymnastics, Donald was proud of soccer — it killed me. And if I ever opened my mouth about how all of this was making me feel, they would say, "Cole, do you not see how much we give you? Are you really that ungrateful?" And I would say, no, no, this has nothing to do with what I have in the physical form! Materialistically, I had everything a child could ever ask for, and yet I still felt without — which at a very young age posed the question, "Where does one find fulfillment?" Anything my parents gave me didn't feel like mine. That desk wasn't mine. My own bedroom wasn't mine. The only thing that was mine was my passion, my interests, and those were constantly being attacked. "Cole, there's no future in playing video games. Cole, you should be in the musical! Cole, what about science camp? Cole, French. Cole, med school. Cole, Cole, Cole."

That's the reason I clung to the World of Warcraft. Because

it was mine and mine only. And being prohibited from sharing it gave me even more reason to worship it, because that meant I was doing it for myself and no one else.

My mother said it all the time: "Stewart, from Brooke's violin group? You know how talented he is. Well, I just found out from one of the other moms that his parents don't want him studying violin in college. They force him to stop practicing. Can you believe that? Do they not see their son is the next Itzhak Perlman? I feel so bad for kids like that. If the kid wants to play the violin, let the kid play the violin! Who are they to tell him what he should or shouldn't do? You know what I always say — do what you love!"

Hearing it straight from my mother's mouth like that — the irony! So badly, I wanted to hold a petri dish underneath her words, catch them in their purity, place them under a microscope and show her, "Mom, it's the same thing! Violin, World of Warcraft, they're the *same*. Please, can't you *see?* This is about *expression,* not the thing *itself!*"

When Brooke started learning the violin, we were all expected to attend her recitals, to support her, to never put her down no matter what we thought of the instrument. When Thomas started gymnastics, we were all expected to attend his competitions, to support him, to never put him down no matter what we thought of the sport. When Donald started playing soccer, playing violin and following in Brooke's footsteps, we were all expected to attend his games, his recitals, support him and never put him down, never, not ever. Why? Because these ventures were not ours. They were Brooke's, Thomas's, Donald's. And who were we to decide for them their path in life?

But noooooo, when I wanted to pursue a life of video games, get an internship at Blizzard Entertainment, I had it all mapped out, even shared it with my mother and father thinking they'd get behind my mature perspective and foresight into a possible career path, no, suddenly I was tainting the family image, throwing black in the rainbow, that family law about always supporting each other no matter what flying out the window.

So, you have to understand the rage in me. All those years getting called a fag for dancing in the school show choir, doing the Charleston front and center, honoring my mother and her love for music. All the years of me taking piano lessons, slaving over Mozart and Chopin, fucking Chopin, chords too big for my hands. All the afternoon violin recitals I sat through, listening to every age group, first the five year olds, then the six year olds, then the seven year olds, then the eight year olds, *Twinkle Twinkle Little Star*, *Mary Had A Little Lamb*, it was mind-numbing, just to support Brooke. All the afternoons I parked it in the bleachers, watching Thomas and a million other nine year old boys run around in spandex, jumping from event to event, trying my best not to make Thomas feel like I didn't want to be there, which was against the law, and the law said we supported each other no matter what. But when I wanted to do this thing here that I loved, really loved — I wasn't even asking for them to understand it, learn it, play it with me; all I wanted was to be given the freedom to explore it by myself — instead, they called it unhealthy, said I was addicted, that ten years from now I'd look back in regret and say, "I wish I hadn't wasted my teenage years playing that stupid video game."

But was I crazy? Was I the only human being in the world who found value in playing video games? Obviously not. There were close to three million people playing World of Warcraft at the time, and the overwhelming consensus was that this passion of ours had to be hidden. We were all in love with the game, and we were all chastised for it.

[Party][Ez]: It's just absurd to me that society celebrates shit like baseball and reality television, but here I am, child of Satan for playing a fucking video game.

[Party][Maull]: Whoever invented reality TV needs to be burned at the stake.

[Party][Ez]: I look at someone hitting a home run and I'm like, ok, that takes skill, I obviously can't do that, so I applaud them. But then these fuckers turn around and are like, "Oh, you sit at home and play video games all day, that must be really fucking hard."

[Party][Ez]: It's such cockery. I'd like to see them handle a Molten Core raid with forty health bars and bomb timers on their screen with a guild leader screaming in their ear.

[Party][Clitauren]: Did you just turn cock into a verb?

[Party][Ez]: Sure did. Action verb, s0n.

[Party][Clitauren]: I'm going to use that with the next girl I hook up with. "Sup baby, up for some cockery?"

[Party][Maull]: Landon, be honest, when was the last time you got laid.

[Party][Clitauren]: Idk, ask your sister.

[Party][Ez]: LOL REKT

[Party][Maull]: You know what I find hilarious? My sister and mom both HATE the fact that I play WoW, but when their computer breaks, suddenly I'm the lord and savior of the family.

[Party][Ez]: Dude. So fucking true.

[Party][Clitauren]: My mom is the same way. She whines so much about how much time I spend on the computer, but then she needs me to hold her hand opening a web browser to search for cooking recipes on Google.

[Party][Maull]: Haha, I thought I was the only one who had to deal with that.

[Party][Ez]: I'm pretty sure behind every single WoW player is a pissed off mother who wishes her son would be more like Zac Efron.

[Party][Clitauren]: *Swoops bangs in front of eyes* ACCEPT ME FOR WHO I AM, MOM.

[Party][Maull]: Who the fuck is Zac Efron?

[Party][Ez]: How do you not know who Zac Efron is...

[Party][Maull]: Uhhh, cuz I have a ballsack?

[Party][Clitauren]: He's this retardedly good looking fellow on the Disney channel who may or may not enjoy taking a tip in his butthole every now and then.

[Party][Maull]: Ok so my first question here would be why the fuck are you watching the Disney channel

[Party][Clitauren]: Bro, my sister has it on like 23 hours a day, I hear it from the other room.

[Party][Maull]: Uh huh, sure.

[Party][Ez]: The other day my English teacher overheard me and this kid talking about WoW, and she told us that "Warcraft World" was a dangerous game and I got so mad. Mostly because I haven't slept in three months. But still.

[Party][Clitauren]: Dude this girl in my class calls it that too. What the fuck is with people calling it Warcraft World? It's fucking World of Warcraft. How hard is that to remember?

[Party][Ez]: Well, when you consider the fact that most of our country can recognize the McDonald's logo but doesn't know the name of our current president, it seems pretty reasonable to me.

[Party][Maull]: And people wonder why I prefer to spend my time on the Internet...

[Party][Ez]: Right dude?

[Party][Maull]: The real world is full of fucking retards.

[Party][Clitauren]: Who then call us retards.

[Party][Ez]: Brb killing myself.

I wanted to believe that somehow I would find a way to make it all work, convince my parents that World of Warcraft was a digital mirror of all other esteemed crafts in life, that it was the *perfect* venue for their eldest son, imprisoned by the bathroom and

100

consequent inept member of society, to nurture his potential as a leader. Surely they would be able to draw the parallel. They would be so proud. They would say, on Oprah, my story would spread that far, "You know, at first, we didn't understand, but we like to think of ourselves as open-minded parents. We really only want the best for our son. So one night we sat down, all of us (on the show my mother would reach over and grab my father's hand), and had us a good long talk about it. And of course we had our doubts, as any loving parents would, but he explained himself very well — our son is so articulate. How this video game was actually a living metaphor for real life, taught many of the same lessons, was quite valuable to a boy who was sick all the time and didn't leave the house much. And even though we didn't completely understand, because, well, we didn't grow up with computers, didn't have all these things when we were his age, still, we knew he was a good kid, and if this made him happy then who were we to stop him?"

But every time I tried to detail the similarities between striving to complete a quest and striving to learn a new song on the piano, my parents would laugh at my stupidity, shake their heads and say, "Cole, can you not see how this game is pulling you in? Look at you. You're losing touch with reality. You're becoming an addict."

When my siblings shared their metaphors though, what brilliance! "Mom, isn't it neat how studying for a math test is kind of like practicing for hours and hours to learn a new song on the violin?" My parents clapped and squealed and raised their glasses in approval — they had the wisest children in all the land.

And what was the result of all this positive reinforcement? My siblings became masters, leaders, idolized figurines. Brooke was accepted into the most prestigious youth symphony orchestra in Chicago. Thomas was one of the only eight-year-old gymnasts in the nation to receive a perfect score on parallel bars in a tournament, immediately declared Olympic bound by coaches across the country. And Donald? He had his interests, but his real gift was nurtured by being last on my parents' priority list. They were so busy obsessing over me, and paying very close attention to

101

Brooke, and staying on top of Thomas, that much of what Donald did went unnoticed, until he spoke up at the dinner table, seven years old, with a proverb that could only marinate in a soul of a thousand years: "Who are we, to blow out each other's candles in an attempt to make ours shine brighter?" And my parents, my mother especially, would clasp her hand over her mouth, and through a clenched throat of pride squeeze out, "My baby!"

It was infuriating! For the life of me, I could not figure out why my parents, my family, the entire world preached open-mindedness, diversity of interests, the value of new technology, and, at the same time, looked down upon the World of Warcraft.

After much deliberation, I could come to only one logical answer:

Make them hear you.

In the real world, it was simple: you could hear the notes on the violin becoming more polished, you could see the gymnastics routine getting cleaner, you could taste the more expensive steak, smell the new car, fall asleep in the bigger bed — success was all so visceral. The only way for a parent to know if their child, their masterpiece, was moving in the right direction, was to see it grow taller, think faster, speak more eloquently and collect verified achievements.

If I wanted them to understand my passion, respect it, support my pursuit, then I had to prove its worth. And the only way I could prove its worth was to achieve some sort of tangible success. It had to be seen. It had to have meaning. I had to become someone so iconic in the gaming world that even people in the real world would take notice. My character had to be flawless.

Then they would understand. Then they would be proud.

Every day and every night, I held that image in my vision, imagining myself achieving undeniable fame and fortune in the World of Warcraft. I dreamt of the day I would calmly walk downstairs to the kitchen and beckon my family to come look, come upstairs and see. Apprehensive, they would follow, and as I took my seat in my computer chair, they would form a half moon behind me. On my screen, my Mage would stand, clothed in colorful robes, fiery shoulders, a decorated headpiece and glowing staff in hand — such obvious proof that the character on my screen was an extrinsic representation of the disciplined and persistent boy sitting in his gym shorts and wrinkled T-shirt behind the keyboard. They would stare at my screen and patiently listen to my explanation. And finally, the puzzle pieces of this foreign endeavor would come together for them.

My siblings would smile and my mother's eyes would wet with pride, and my father would reach out and place his large hands on my shoulders. I would be exhausted from the journey, my eyelids heavy and my stomach growling, but in that moment, it would all be worth it.

My family would say, in unison:

"Cole, we support you no matter what."

And I would be free, because they loved me for me.

Chapter 6
Remember The Name

How far was I willing to go to prove that World of Warcraft was a worthwhile endeavor?

The last week of my Honor grind, I was 200,000 Honor points short of hitting Rank 10. All I had to do was stay home from school one more day, just one more day, and I would hit my cap on Tuesday. I timed everything perfectly. I hinted at flu-like symptoms during dinner, Sunday evening. I made it a point to clutch my stomach a few times during flashcards with Dad after dinner. At exactly 9:58 p.m., moments before my mother peeked her head into my domain to see if I was tucked in for bed, I planted myself in the bathroom. Knowing she would come looking for me, I waited for her nighttime voice just outside the door — "Cole, are you in there?" — to which I responded, lightly, tiredly, clenched in pain — "Yeah Mom, *I'm in here.*" I could practically hear her heart breaking!

[Mom]: "Oh no... How are you feeling?"

[Me]: "Not good, Mom."

(And then a pause.)

[Me]: "*Not good.*"

[Mom]: "Can I get you anything? Maybe a hot washcloth to put on your tummy?"

[Me]: "It's ok. I'll be fine. *Don't worry about me.*"

I was sitting on the toilet, the lid down, my shorts still on, but my head in my hands to ensure I did not break character.

[Mom]: "Oh sweetie…"

It was perfect! All of it, perfect! I swear, no one, not a single child on the face of this earth could fake sick with the same dramatism, the same commitment to the craft. When I was done, I pretended to wipe, the sound of the toilet paper roll spinning on its rod, the whooshing cardboard and the delicate fall of each ply into the water below, just in case my mother had decided to sit outside the door and wait, wait to see if the scene was all she'd imagined, wait to spot my inadequacies as an actor. But mother! You taught me so well! Even if you were in another state, another country, another world, still would I have executed my motions with the same precision, if for no other reason than to ensure the bad habit of negligence never arose in the first place.

When twenty minutes had passed and a moderate stomach ache had appeared to have taken place, I walked down the hallway to give my mother and father an update: clutching my stomach, hanging my head, yes mom and dad, *it happened again*. My mother sat up in her king size bed with six fluffy pillows around her and wrapped me into her arms, to which I fell like a dead corpse. My father, with his one pillow, pushed himself up with one arm and looked over, before pulling his nightshade over his eyes and saying, "Feel better. I need to go to sleep. I have an early surgery in the morning." Reluctantly, although purposefully, I removed myself from my mother's embrace and she said, "I'm sure you'll feel better in the morning. Go get some rest. I love you." And to complete the scene I, a child whose life was hanging on a thread, limped my way out of their room, my whispers being thrown behind me, "I love you too, Mom. Goodnight. Goodnight, Dad."

I closed their bedroom door —

— and then I made a run for it.

Back to my computer! There was no time to waste. I stayed up until 5:00 a.m. grinding Honor points. If I wasn't on the brink of insomnia-induced death before, I certainly was now. My eyes were red hot. My stare was in and out of focus. My consciousness could no longer tell if the World of Warcraft was the dream world and this bedroom of mine was real, or if it was the other way around. My walls looked strange, as if closing in on me. My door looked warped and out of focus. My window glowed with God — wait, never mind, just the rising sun.

When my morning alarm rang, I jolted up in bed. I had only slept an hour, but I was full of false energy. I still had one last scene to execute if I were to be granted the gift of staying home from school.

I could hear my father's footsteps just down the hall, making his way from the front banister to the kitchen. Strategically, I meandered down the back banister, haunting my way into the kitchen from the opposite direction. There, I could see him in the corner by the coffee maker, equally as tired, pouring himself a fresh cup and then holding it up to his nose, as if hoping the aroma itself would give him the life he sought.

[Me]: "Dad?"

He practically dropped the coffee mug, turning around quickly to see who was there.

[Dad]: "Cole? What are you doing up so early?"

[Me]: "*I... Feel... So... Sick....*"

[Dad]: "Seriously? Again?"

[Me]: "Dad, I feel *awful*."

[Dad]: "That's it, I'm taking you in to see somebody."

[Me]: "No, no Dad. I just need to go upstairs. I need to sleep. That's all. I'm sure it's just the flu."

[Dad]: "Fine. Go upstairs. I'll have mom call the nurse."

I had to keep from running to my room in excitement! On

this Monday, my dream would be realized. On this Monday, I would finish collecting the remainder of the Honor points needed for Rank 10. On this Monday, I would secure my fate in the World of Warcraft. And tomorrow, I would reap my rewards, and then, then, I would be free!

I set my alarm for 8:15 a.m., fifteen minutes after both my parents would be off to work. Then I celebrated by diving under my covers and immediately passing out.

[Mom]: "Cole, wake up."

I groaned, turning over in my bed.

[Me]: "Mom, I'm sick. I already talked to Dad. He said you'd call the nurse."

[Mom]: "Yeah, you've been sick a lot lately."

She said it in an accusatory way. She was on to me.

[Me]: "But Mom, I really don't feel well!"

She ripped off my covers, threw them on the floor, and then walked back into the hallway, shouting behind her.

[Mom]: "Sometimes, we all have to do things we don't want to do!"

Someone please, point to the mistake I had made! Show me where in my performance I had once, even for a single second, revealed the boy behind the character — because even in my own mind, I could not see him! Oh, but I was not going to roll over so easily. I threw on some clothes, ran downstairs and jumped into the sickest, most broken character I had ever portrayed. Wobbling, groaning, grabbing my stomach, every trick in the book was showcased in hopes of pleasing my audience.

[Me]: "Mom, I can't. I feel like I'm going to throw up. My throat hurts. I think I have a fever. Seriously, it feels like I'm dying. Mom, maybe I should see a doctor after all. It's so bad. Please. Pleaseeeeeee. I *have* to stay home today."

I was begging for my life. I couldn't make it another week. If I didn't hit Rank 10 tomorrow, it was over. I felt weak and I was hungry and I craved my bed, craved it to the point where, during what little time I allowed myself to sleep, I would dream of sleeping and the pleasures of pillows.

[Mom]: "Save it, Cole. Nobody gets this sick, this often. Nobody. You're going to school and that's that."

I had to think of a plan. Something. Anything to keep me home! Grinding Honor points tonight wouldn't be enough to hit my cap. I needed the entire day.

The only thing I knew would convince my mother was if she could see the sickness. I had to prove it to her. So I did what any other boy in my position would have done.

I went into the bathroom to make myself throw up.

I closed the door and stood over the toilet. I looked down. I'd never stared at a toilet bowl before, really stared. I was always facing the other direction, trapped on the seat, looking outward at the world, but now? Now, I was staring down the rabbit hole itself, and it never seemed to end. The toilet bowl just went on and on.

Oblivious to my own affliction, to exactly just how far I was willing to go for success in the World of Warcraft, I lifted the toilet seat, aimed my head over the bowl, and proceeded to stick my finger down my throat, poking at the dangly thing in the back. My stomach dry-heaved, my face pulled tight with trauma. My body begged me to stop. I had deprived it of every necessity, and now I was asking it to spit up what little bit was left.

My first attempt was a failure. I couldn't vomit. I hated what I knew was coming, the release of liquid food and stomach acids up my chest and through my mouth. But it had to be done. It was the only way. I tried again. I poked at the back of my throat, heaving up nothing but air. Hands on my thighs, I panted, a tear running down my cheek from the shock of it, spitting the taste of my fingers into the toilet.

From the kitchen, my mother yelled.

[Mom]: "Come on, Cole! It's time to go!"

This was my last chance. Three months of hard work would be for nothing if I didn't make it to Rank 10. I needed those last two pieces of gear. Otherwise, my Mage would look like a chop-shop special, wearing only half the armor, looking like at the last minute I'd given up.

I refused to give up.

One last time, I took my pointer finger and jammed it down my throat. My stomach heaved so violently that my face felt like it was ripping apart. My eyes squeezed shut and my mouth gagged open, the back of my throat seizing as I poked for something, anything to come up and act as proof to my mother that I was sick. I was really, truly sick.

Over and over again, I dry-heaved into the toilet. My stomach was completely empty. I was asking my body to give me something it didn't have. I spat into the toilet a couple times, flushed, and then walked out of the bathroom, defeated. I'd failed.

I climbed into my mom's minivan and rode to school. My head hurt from the torture I'd put myself through.

During third period, a kid next to me said, "Cole, what's wrong with your face?"

I thought he was just being an asshole, picking on me for no reason.

"It looks like you have a rash or something," he said.

I raised my hand and excused myself to the bathroom. In the mirror, I assessed the damage. In trying to make myself throw up, I'd dry-heaved so violently that hundreds of tiny blood vessels had popped all over my forehead and cheeks. It was worse than a rash. I looked like a monster.

For the rest of the day, I fended off rumors that I'd fallen face-first into poison ivy. I made up some excuse about how I was allergic to the fabric softener used to wash my pillowcases. I told my mom and dad the same thing at the dinner table. My mom immediately ran upstairs and threw the detergent away.

When I sat down at my computer after school the next day, Tuesday, I took a deep breath and stared at the World of Warcraft log in screen for a long moment. This was it. My eyes were bloodshot, my throat was raw, I had red dots all over my face, I was starving, and all I wanted to do was go to sleep. If I didn't make it, I was done. Done, you hear me? Done!

I opened my Honor tab, and there it was, the final declaration. I was inches away from Rank 10. I had barely missed it, just barely. One more week and I would have it for sure. One more week. I let that thought settle. Seven more days of Battlegrounds. Seven more days of number crunching. Seven more days of headaches and paranoia and dragging myself from class to class without enough energy to communicate effectively, sometimes falling asleep for a second or two right there in the hallway, mid step. Seven more days of insanity.

I couldn't do it. I'd hit rock bottom. One more week and I would die.

I quit the Honor grind at Rank 9 ½. I was no Champion.

So. Fine. I admit it. Ok? I'm admitting it, Mom and Dad! The World of Warcraft was not some casual after-school activity or a way for me to "unwind." It was not conducive to my well being, my sleep schedule, or my emotional state. It was, in every way, an unhealthy demand that I thrust upon myself, and was a futile course of action with no meaningful resolve. You were right, I was wrong. It's just, I guess, well…

I guess you could say, Dad, it was a lot like how I imagine medical school was for you. Binging on espresso in the doctor's lounge between observations. Falling asleep in your dinner after not being home for three days. Enslaving yourself to the grind, and for what? Fun? The joy of a white lab coat? Do not deny the motivation a bright red BMW dangling in the white horizon can have on a young graduate, father. Actually, wasn't it your own father who had questioned your ability to become a doctor? Sheesh, I can only imagine. Seeking his approval like a coal miner in search of light. Living in the library. Abandoning your social youth for a dream. Wiping old people's bottoms (as you'd told me too many times) at the local nursing home in an effort to beef up your resumé...so that one day you could help people walk again? Possibly. But let us also acknowledge the desire each of us humans enlisted in reward-driven societies has to possess a title that says, "In this game of life, I am a player of value."

And you, Mom. Daughter of a drill sergeant. How many clubs did you join? How many committees did you lead? I know you love this story because you tell it all the time. It shows your commitment! When the world (to a daughter, isn't her father The World?) said you couldn't, you wouldn't be able to, what did you do? You proved him wrong! He said, "Fine. I'll let you go to Disney World with your dance team at the end of the year. But only if you become Captain." Weeks, you worked. Nights, you didn't sleep. Heartache for approval was your bearing. And for what? Was dangling Disney World the impetus of your relentless drive and commitment? Possibly. But let us also acknowledge the lengths a child will go to show his or her parents what their deepest love means to them. A title that says, "In this game of life, I am a player of value."

So, look. I'm sorry. I'm telling you now, Mom and Dad, out in the open. During my sophomore year of high school, and for many years after that, I violated every single one of your family laws. I lied to you. I cut corners. I forfeited food and sleep and I poured myself into a game for a title that said, "I am a player of value." That's all I wanted. I was simply a soul stirring with ambition, trapped inside a body chained to the bathroom. You had engraved in me the same drive and unquenchable ambition that had propelled both of you to greatness. Except I didn't know how to be that in real life — or I knew, but was physically incapable. So I explored the only road available to me at the time.

Because I wanted to be just like you.

Despite my failure to achieve the Rank 10 title of Champion, The Honor grind taught me a very important life lesson — the very lesson that both of you too often orated at the dinner table. The four months I spent grinding Honor in my zombie state of stupor demanded more of me than the eleven years I'd spent playing piano and the ten years I'd spent playing hockey, combined. Never had I pushed myself so far past the point of failure. Never had I felt that hollow feeling of true commitment. I hit rock bottom so hard that by the time I called it quits, I was emotionally naked, stripped to the core. And in that fragile, vulnerable state, I was, for the first time as an extremely insecure adolescent, able to see the depth of my own potential.

When all was said and done, I didn't need to hit Rank 14, or even Rank 10 to feel validated. The lesson, the real reward, was the revelation of my work ethic. I saw what I was capable of, as a person, and it raised the standard I held for myself.

The way I approached the game thereafter was very different. So much of my day was spent hiding my time online that I needed a reason, a very good reason, to continue risking what few privileges I had just to play World of Warcraft. I couldn't raid. I couldn't devote enough time to the Honor grind to achieve a prestigious rank. I wasn't satisfied with playing for fun, no different than how I had been unsatisfied playing hockey unless I was en route to the NHL. I needed to be the best. But if by the game's standards becoming "the best" was impossible, then why continue playing? Why fight for a game that would lead nowhere?

I started to question my desires for these epic items and prestigious ranks, and with that questioning came the quiet thought that maybe I didn't need them after all — maybe I didn't need a title. During my Honor grind, I had acquired enough gear to hold my own on the battlefield. Nothing great, nothing that would warrant praise from other players, but enough to survive a few strong attacks, giving me a small window of opportunity to outplay my opponent and potentially come out on top.

I indulged in this idea of seeing my value as a player in terms of my own ability, opposed to the rewards we as players were told to acquire — and inevitably defined us. When looking at the lavishly decorated, I began to see beyond their appearance, and behind it, a great disconnect. Some of the highest ranked, materialistically valuable players were complacent beneath the surface. Their unsharpened skills slowly depreciated over time. And if I could survive the initial shock of the power they wielded — single attacks taking out huge chunks of my health bar — then an opportunity would eventually arise to take control of the situation and defeat them. Gear, although a tremendous force in the World of Warcraft, was not the end-all. Skill, I believed, could prevail.

I started spending my time in the World of Warcraft honing this idea. I sought out the best players on my server, the ones in all epics, the Rank 12's, Rank 13's, Rank 14's, and challenged them relentlessly. I taunted them into dueling me again and again. If I lost, I swallowed their mockery and dug deeper into my practice. Another duel, another chance to learn.

Rathorse. Stanuar. Wildes. Soot. Jefreestar. Thwong. Chauvanist. Redux. Glorin. Dw. Ras. Frijolero. Sheepy. Ig. Wonka. Nofear. Joebo. Facehugger. Zapatos. Myztery. Niniveve. Tacitus. Mcstub. Fukumi. Toysrus. Emptyquiver. Aoedaosi. Curssiu. Sonya. Theads. Tj. Grundle. Zyx. Whalen. Margorah. Groinshot. Snuffy. Murda. Teeku. Neophyte. Whiteknight. Forcemaster. Rankawesome. Coffeeman. Engineer. Glaise. Maull. Clitauren. Even Ez. I practiced against them all. Every top player on Wildhammer that had made a name for themselves acted as my teacher. Most of these players were hardcore gamers, having played online games for much longer than I and came from worlds like Everquest, Runescape, and Dota. These were players that, if caught on the losing side of a battle, would leave their computers and do a lap around the house to avoid smashing their keyboard into a million bits. These were Wildhammer's finest, and while I was severely out-geared in comparison, slowly but surely, I earned my place among them.

To supplement my rigorous practice, I spent at least an hour a day on a website called WarcraftMovies, where players posted videos of themselves playing our beloved game. The most popular videos were often made by players that had achieved success as it was formally defined, sporting the Rank 14 title or a gluttonous costume of epic gear. But there was one Mage, one player that stood out to me despite not having either.

His name was Cachexic.

His character moved with a rhythm and flow other Mages lacked. There was never any hesitation in his execution, each ability flowing into the next. The way he approached the World of Warcraft was an art.

Intrigued as to how I could adopt a similar play style, I made a Level 1 character on his server, Frostmane, one of the original WoW servers launched at the same time as Stormreaver.

[Cacklealt]: Hey, you busy?

[Cachexic]: What's up.

[Cacklealt]: Haha, didn't expect you to respond

[Cacklealt]: Just wanted to say that I'm a big fan of your videos

[Cachexic]: Thanks.

[Cacklealt]: Do you think you could teach me some of your tricks?

[Cacklealt]: I really want to learn

[Cachexic]: What sort of tricks?

[Cacklealt]: I dunno, anything really

[Cacklealt]: I feel like you play differently than most people I've seen, and I'd like to learn how

[Cachexic]: There aren't really any tricks to playing a Mage.

[Cachexic]: I think it's just something you soak up. I've been lucky to play with and against some great players.

That's when it clicked. Wildhammer had gotten me this far, but I was quickly outgrowing my competition. If I wanted to become the best, if I was really committed to this craft, then I needed a true mentor. I needed to be back on a Day 1 server where intense competition would shape me into the player I knew I could become.

[Cacklealt]: Do you think if I made a character on your server, you'd be willing to teach me?

[Cacklealt]: I'm not some creep, I promise lol. I just really want to get better at playing a Mage.

[Cachexic]: You're going to level a new Mage here?

[Cacklealt]: Sure, why not

[Cachexic]: To level 60?

[Cacklealt]: Yeah

I hadn't thought the whole thing through yet. I just wanted to see what he would say.

[Cachexic]: Sure kid.

[Cachexic]: If you level a Mage to 60 here, I'll teach you.

[Cachexic]: But my guess is you'll quit somewhere around level 30. Those levels suck.

It had been almost two years since I'd started playing World of Warcraft. I'd achieved much of what I'd set out for. But along the way, something had changed for me. I stopped seeing the World of Warcraft as a means to an end. The game had become my slow and steady disposition, my daily practice. It wasn't about achieving something inside the game anymore. What I wanted was to be remembered as a truly incredible, creative player.

116

Compelled by nothing more than a gut feeling, I decided to risk everything. I logged back over to my Mage on Wildhammer and said my goodbyes.

Cachexic would be my teacher. I would be his apprentice.

To ensure that I would not give up on this arduous path, I removed the option all together and deleted my Level 60 Mage, Cackle. The one I had just spent four months working on.

And for the third time, I started all the way back at Level 1.

I named myself Firephunk.

Now, tell me. Is this the decision a video game addict makes?

Does a child that simply can't handle a screenless afternoon and its consequential sober itch throw away his character for no immediate gain or reward? Does a child that lives with a glossy haze in his eyes from snorting the blood of the Alliance find enjoyment in giving up his trivial fame and fortune? Does a child who uses World of Warcraft as nothing more than an efficient escape from the hell of his own reality really possess the discipline, any discipline at all, to embark on a costly quest for the unlikely chance of being mentored by a more talented player?

No. No, he does not.

I was not an addict. I was a pro in the making.

It took me another four months to level a new Undead Mage to level 60. Four months of grinding experience points late into the night. Four months of playing entirely by myself. Every once in a while, I would hop into the old Ventrilo channel with Marve, Sam, and Landon, and we'd talk while I leveled my new Mage. But for the most part, I was alone, motivated only by the thought of getting to learn firsthand from one of the greatest Mages I'd ever seen play the game.

At the same time, I had quite a bit of making up to do in

school. The Honor grind had left my grade point average in a state of disarray, and every night at the dinner table my parents expressed their fury.

[Dad]: "If I were bringing home grades like this, I'd be working my tail off to make sure my résumé was chalk full of activities."

[Mom]: "That's how I got into University of Illinois, you know. I didn't have the best grades — they were good, not stellar. But I was involved in so many extracurricular activities, the school saw what a hard worker I was and decided to let me in. That's what you need to be doing, Cole."

But what about my stomach aches! The gurgling in my abdomen and the constant sprinting for the bathroom! Would a club really welcome me and all my stench, Mother?

[Dad]: "This is a big semester for you. You're turning 16. You're getting your driver's license and driving is a privilege you have to earn. If you want to drive one of my expensive cars then I expect to see some real effort from you in school."

[Mom]: "We've talked about this before, Cole. You're not playing hockey anymore. We let you spend all the time you wanted on your computer last semester. It's time to get back on track here."

All the time I wanted?

[Dad]: "I'll make you a deal. By Monday of next week, you find a club to join that will supplement your résumé."

[Me]: "And what do I get in return?"

[Mom]: "What you get, Cole, is the benefit of us steering you down the right path so that when it comes time to apply to college, you'll be a candidate worth considering."

[Dad]: "And when you turn 16, we'll see about you getting your license."

I let out a big sigh. One of those teenager sighs.

118

[Me]: "I'll try my best."

[Mom]: "I bet you'll start trying real hard when we take away that computer of yours."

I said fine. Whatever.

One club.

But that's it.

And I was on my way to the yearbook committee informational meeting after school, I swear I was, but then all of a sudden, it was the weirdest thing, my stomach dropped, just dropped out of nowhere. So I couldn't go.

The radio club sounded pretty cool; we had a studio by the science hallway with microphones and everything, but they met Tuesdays and Thursdays at 5:30 a.m. and that just wasn't going to work with my schedule.

Student elections were coming up. I thought about running for president. "VOTE FOR COLE! HE'S GOT SOUL!" But Roger Johnson was running too. He was the starting quarterback. I watched him work during lunch, making his rounds to all the tables, shaking hands, his blonde hair like a jar of honey to the buzzing girls. I was seated with a few kids from my math class, the ones that weren't quite athletes and weren't quite popular and weren't quite much of anything — misfits. We weren't even friends, just bodies we could surround ourselves with so none of us would have to bear the burden of being seen eating alone. Roger came by our table and gave us his pitch: "Do you guys think we deserve the best Turnabout Dance this school has ever seen? Vote for me!" He'd made buttons. I took a button. I didn't wear it, but I had it in my pocket. He was going to win for sure.

Jazz Band? I auditioned. With a classical piece: *Lotus Land*, by Cyril Scott. Very modern. Stormy and beautiful. I was not selected. They picked a kid who could play Chopsticks in a flashy, jazzy way. Which was fine.

I walked down the empty hallways after school to room 14C and took a seat at one of the desks. There were five others: three girls and the one guy in our grade who was openly gay. He was practicing a monologue by himself in the corner, pressing his black chapeau in his hand to his chest while waving his other hand in the air in front of him. Very dramatic.

The teacher walked in.

[Mr. Wagner]: "Welcome, all! To this semester's Speech Team try outs!"

One by one, we were called into the room across the hall.

Mr. Wagner shut the door and sat in a chair a few feet in front of me, all the desks pushed to the perimeter, creating a mini stage.

[Mr. Wagner]: "And what will you be performing?"

I hadn't really practiced. Picked it last minute. I'd done hundreds, thousands of scenes in the kitchen for my mother and my family. I stood in the center of the room and pretended I was in the kitchen. I impersonated Stewie from *Family Guy*. I thought I was pretty good.

[Me]: *"Tired of not being able to find clothes that fit? I know I was That's why I started Stewie's Big and Tall Man Shop. If you're portly or tall, you'll find a friendly atmosphere brimming with personalized and expert service. 'Hey Stewie, how's the weather up there?' Very fair — like our prices."*

Mr. Wagner's face lit up.

I made the speech team.

[Mom]: "The speech team? That's fantastic, Cole! You were a born performer — you are *so* my son. What a perfect club for you! You get to perform, you get to collaborate with others — Original Comedy is totally your game. You make us all laugh here at home! This is so, so wonderful. Think about how much you're

120

going to learn! I can say from experience that clubs and school organizations taught me so much. They taught me how to take a project and run with it, how to really dig into the work. And I learned a ton about other people! Really, there is no greater experience than learning how to work toward a final performance. That's something any job recruiter will be able to recognize. They'll tell the kid with straight A's: 'No, sorry, we're going to go with Cole over here because Cole knows how to get stuff done!' Think about it. What's the one thing all businesses care about, Cole? Goals. If you can help them achieve their goal, well then you just watch how fast you work your way up that ladder. And what an incredible way to learn these life lessons, doing what you love! The speech team! You're going to acquire so many valuable skills. And you know what? You'll be able to apply those skills to every other aspect of your life. Believe me, colleges, future hirers, they will absolutely draw the parallel and value your experience. Not to say that you should only be doing this to get ahead in the world! You know what I always say: Live what you love, and be the guy who gets paid to do it! You must be so excited about this opportunity, because you'll get to do both! I mean, Original Comedy, I can just imagine all the things this could lead to. Maybe you'll become a performer like me! Not that I'm saying you have to; it's your life; in fact you shouldn't — you should find your own thing — as long as it makes you happy! I'm just saying, as your mother, my only hope is to see you live the life you envision for yourself. And this seems like it will! Oh it definitely will. I can't wait to see you perform! When can we? I'll bring the whole family. The whole family is coming! We would all love that. Because what do we do in this family? That's right. We support each other no matter what. And this is absolutely something we all support. And who cares what anyone else thinks! Right? Who cares if none of the 'cool kids' think the speech team is all that great. Screw 'em! They don't know how talented you are. They don't know who you're going to be in ten years. Do what you love and ignore the rest of them! Just remember, Cole. At the end of the day, even if everyone in the world says what you're doing is stupid, or worthless, or a waste of time, you'll always have your mama there, front and center, cheering you on. Because — and you know I say this all the time but as your mother I have to say it again — sometimes it's not always about the activity itself, but what it teaches you. That's why I support this no matter what. The lessons you'll learn are the real reward!"

Sitting there at the dinner table, drawing the parallel between the speech team and the World of Warcraft, I wanted to slowly insert my butter knife up my nasal cavity until it punctured my brain and I died face first into my spaghetti (wheat).

On the day I finally reached level 60, I immediately messaged Cachexic.

[Firephunk] whispers: Guess what

[Firephunk] whispers: I did it!

[Cachexic] whispers: Well would you look at that.

[Cachexic] whispers: Have to hand it to ya, kid. I didn't think you were actually serious about leveling a Mage here.

[Firephunk] whispers: Haha, thanks. I told you!

[Cachexic] whispers: You kept your end of the bargain, looks like I need to keep mine.

[Cachexic] whispers: I'm here in The Badlands waiting for our raid to start. I'll have a friend summon you. We can duel a few times for fun.

Cachexic invited me to a group and had a Warlock from his guild summon me to the area. Cachexic was standing by himself right outside of town. His shoulders glowed orange, and in his right hand was his brand new Rank 14 High Warlord staff. In the four months it had taken me to level to 60, he'd finished his own Honor grind and achieved the highest status in the game. He looked invincible.

[Firephunk] whispers: Congrats on Rank 14 man.

[Cachexic] whispers: Thanks. I hit it last Tuesday and I've

literally slept 15 hours a day since.

[Cachexic] whispers: This is my first real day back.

Cachexic has challenged you to a duel.

[Firephunk] whispers: My gear sucks haha

[Cachexic] whispers: Gear doesn't matter.

Yes, Cachexic was indeed the wise teacher I believed him to be, and this was my chance to show him that I was worthy of being trained.

Your duel will begin in 3... 2... 1....

I chased him down. He started casting Sheep, and I Counterspelled. But he'd canceled his cast a millisecond before, faking my counter. He hit me with a low-rank Frostbolt, slowing me. Then he ran in and out of range, casting Scorch and retreating, over and over again. I couldn't get a single cast off. He was toying with me. He could have killed me in three seconds, but he didn't. He was making me run around. Others came to watch. The duel ended with him still at full health.

Cachexic has defeated Firephunk in a duel!

Never had I seen someone play with such fluidity. Dueling him was like trying to smash water.

[Firephunk] whispers: Well that was awful.

[Cachexic] whispers: Don't worry about it.

[Firephunk] whispers: Again?

[Cachexic] whispers: Sure, kid.

Your duel will begin in 3... 2... 1...

This time was worse. Same with the three duels after that. And with each loss, whatever ego I had brought with me from Wildhammer, believing myself to be this high and mighty player, began to dissolve. Facing off against Cachexic showed me just how little I really knew about being a Mage.

[Firephunk] whispers: I feel really stupid right now

[Cachexic] whispers: Well, to be fair, you did just hit Level 60

[Firephunk] whispers: I know, but I've been playing a Mage for a while

[Cachexic] whispers: That's what you came here to learn though, right?

[Firephunk] whispers: Right.

[Cachexic] whispers: We're about to do a quick Molten Core raid for a few new guildies. You want to come?

[Firephunk] whispers: Really?

[Cachexic] whispers: Sure. Think of it as a congrats for hitting Level 60. We'll try to get you some Arcanist Bracers or something.

[Firephunk] whispers: Wow, thanks.

[Cachexic] whispers: Here's the guild Ventrilo info. Hop in whenever. Raid starts in fifteen.

My dad yelled upstairs that he was home with Chinese food. Every Friday night, Chinese food. I ran downstairs, loaded up my plate, poured myself a massive glass of orange juice, and then excused myself for the night. Since it was Friday, I was allowed to do that.

I walked back up to my room, set my plate and glass down on my desk, put on my headset and joined the Ventrilo channel.

"That must be Firephunk. Hey Firephunk, this is Cachexic." He sounded older. Cool. Confident.

I got way, way too excited. I'd watched every one of

124

Cachexic's PvP videos countless times. I was a huge fan.

"Hey! Great to finally meet you!"

"Christ, this kid really is a fanboy," said a harsh and raspy voice.

"And that's Sik, our hospitable guild leader," said Cachexic. "Pardon his expletives."

"Fuck no you won't be pardoning shit. Listen up, Firefag. I don't care if you're Cachexic's little butt-buddy or whatever the fuck, just don't get in the way."

Sik sounded like a drill sergeant. I imagined him sitting at his computer in full camo, dog tags around his neck, a beer in his left hand, computer mouse in his right, with a pit bull on the ground gnawing on the leg of a deer.

"Jesus, Sik." Cachexic was laughing.

"What? His name is fucking Firephunk and he was in a guild called <Phunky Town>. Firefag, how old are you, and be fucking honest with me."

"Almost 16."

"I didn't ask what age you ALMOST were, I asked how old you fucking are at this moment. Let's try this again. How old are you."

"15," I said, my voice shaky.

"There. See? Your first answer was you not following directions. The second answer is how I expect you to answer. Don't get fucking smart with me."

I started laughing. I couldn't help it. Yes, part of me was nervous and uncomfortable, but the way Sik talked, I felt like he was joking. There were forty people in this Ventrilo channel and he was the main attraction. I could tell by the tone of his voice, drenched in sarcasm and mental whip, and the fact that everyone

125

else started laughing. What made it so funny was that you would never expect someone to take the World of Warcraft this seriously. And yet, here we all were.

"And Jesus Christ Firefag, stop holding down your push-to-talk button when you laugh. You sound like my girlfriend's 13-year-old niece," Sik said.

I laughed even harder, too nervous to realize my finger was still pressing my push-to-talk key.

"Cache, is this seriously who you got? Of all the kids who jerk off to your videos, *this* is the one that decided to come play with you?"

Cachexic took the stage, defending me.

"Yes, Sik. This is who I got. The man, the legend, Firephunk."

"WAIL, HE'S A GAWD DAMN PHUNK WITH THE FIRE," yelled a teenager with an exaggerated southern accent.

"Firephunk, meet Norman," said Cachexic.

"MY NAME AIN'T NO NORMAN, I'M GAWD DAMN REV-NANCE."

"Also known as Revenance," he said.

Revenance was a Rank 13 Undead Priest and Cachexic's best friend online. They had met playing Star Wars Galaxies Online when they were 12 and had been playing games together ever since. Norman's favorite act was to imitate a racist redneck from the south in an exaggerated southern accent.

"Norman shut the fuck up and come give me Fortitude," said Sik.

"HELL NAW I AIN'T GIVEN YEW NOAH FORTITEWDE," yelled Revenance. He had the whole guild laughing.

126

"No, Norman, you are absolutely going to give me Fortitude or I'm going to kick your fucking ass out of this fucking guild."

"Sik, invite Firephunk to the raid," said Cachexic.

"Fuck no I am not inviting Firefag to the raid."

"If Firephunk doesn't go, I don't go," said Cachexic. We'd known each other for ten minutes and he was already sticking up for me.

"Now that's just bullshit," Sik said. "I made you, motherfucker. I got you all those Honor groups. I grinded Warsong Gulch with you until my eyes bled. You owe me."

"I'll help you grind Runecloth later..." said Cachexic.

Sik invited me to the raid group.

"Oh, he's actually coming?" said Revenance.

"Yes, he's coming. He's my god damn Padawan," said Cachexic.

I'd waited my whole life to be the Padawan of a Jedi Master. My childhood dream was coming true.

"When do I get a Padawan?" said Revenance.

"I dunno. Make videos and hope you get famous like me, I guess," said Cachexic.

"What do Padawan's do, exactly?" said Revenance. He was both genuinely intrigued and highly amused.

"I'm not sure yet. We'll figure that out, won't we Firephunk?" said Cachexic.

"We will!" I said, very eager to get started on whatever internship program Cachexic saw fit.

"By the way Firephunk, what's your real name?" said

Cachexic. "I can't keep calling you Firephunk. My older sister is gonna think I'm a child molester talking to a middle schooler on the Internet. Why the fuck did you name your Mage something so dumb anyway?"

"A few friends made alts here with me when I first re-rolled. We all put 'Phunk' in our names."

"Oh I can't wait to hear the other ones," Revenance said.

"Yes, please share, Firefag."

"Well, there was…"

"Was it Fridayphunk? Or Partyphunk? Or Weliketophunk? I'd have tolerated Weliketophunk," said Revenance.

"One was Moophunk, he was a Tauren Druid…"

"Shitty. Next?"

"The other was an Undead Rogue named Sneakyphunk."

"I'll take Sneakyphunk. Is he still available for slaveship?" said Revenance.

"No, they both gave up pretty early on. It was mostly just a joke."

"So I don't get a slave? WHERE IS MY SLAVE?" Revenance yelled.

"Back to my original question. What's your real name, Firephunk?" said Cachexic.

"Cole."

"Cole?"

"Yeah."

"Well, Cole, I'm Jack, but everyone calls me Cache. Even kids at my school call me Cache."

"Nice to officially meet you," I said.

"HI KOWLE," yelled Revenance.

"And you already know Norman," said Cachexic.

"Don't tell Kowlie Polie my real name!"

"He lives at 574 South Davenport..."

"WHAT THE FUCK CACHE."

"I'm just kidding, I don't know where Norman lives. Somewhere in the middle of fuckin' nowhere. Right Norman?"

"Wail, I gots me sum cows in mah backyhard," he said, again in his southern accent. It really was hilarious.

"You do?" I said. I found it so interesting who you got to meet in the World of Warcraft.

"Jesus, no I don't have cows in my backyard. Who do you think I am, a redneck?"

There was a certain lingo that came with the <Beyond Remorse> crowd. The guild was full of personalities maxed out on the volume knob. Asshole, cunt, cocksucker, these words got thrown around like Sunday morning greetings. Whatever locker room talk I had been exposed to playing hockey, this blew it out of the water.

"Alright, everybody shut the fuck up," said Sik. "Roll call. Everybody here? Good. Buff up, and let's head to Blackrock Mountain."

Among the crowd of players decked in epics gear and glowing weapons, my adolescent Undead Mage stood out like a sore thumb. 39 players from <Beyond Remorse> hopped on their epic mounts, and I rode further behind them on my slower, Level 40 mount. When Cachexic saw I was lagging behind, he turned around to ride with me.

"Cache, where the fuck did you go," said Sik, expecting him to be at the front of the pack with him.

"I'm riding with my Padawan."

"God fucking dammit. I finally get you to Rank 14 and you decide to adopt a special needs child."

Cachexic sent me a private message.

[Cachexic] whispers: Don't worry about Sik. He just wants people to know he's in charge.

[Firephunk] whispers: Haha no worries, I'm just happy to be here.

We made our way into Blackrock Mountain, and leapt one after another into the secret portal to Molten Core.

The group prepared for the raid by exchanging items and buffing each other. I was put on water duty, handing out stacks of water to all the healers. Right before pulling the first Molten Giant, Sik suggested we take a picture. For the guild website.

"Everybody line the fuck up. Tauren, get in the back, Undead get in the front. Stayk, I want you lying on the ground like a god damn cow swimsuit model right fucking now."

"Why can't I be the sex-ay model?" said Revenance.

"Because you're not a plus-size Tauren like Stayk," said Sik.

"I'm curvy," said Stayk. He had the stuffy tone of an intellectual. Stayk was in law school.

Sik stood in the middle of the organized raid group as guild leader, and then right before he took the screenshot said, "God fucking damnitt. Firefag is still in <Phunky Town>. He's messing everything up."

Everyone else wore the guld tag, <Beyond Remorse>.

"Invite him to the guild," said Cachexic.

"I am absolutely not inviting that shitbucket to our guild."

[Cachexic] whispers: Leave your guild.

I disbanded <Phunky Town>.

Cachexic has invited you to join <Beyond Remorse>.

[Firephunk] whispers: Are you sure I can join?

[Cachexic] whispers: I'm an Officer. Accept.

You have joined <Beyond Remorse>!

"GOD FUCKING DAMMIT. WHO GAVE CACHEXIC INVITE PRIVILEGES."

"Owned," said Fatehand.

"Wail, Sik. Lewks like Firephunk is here to stay," said Revenance.

"Firefag, I want you to listen very carefully," said Sik.

Ventrilo went quiet.

"I don't know you, I don't want to know you, and in the brief amount of time that I have known you, you've pissed me off with your high-pitched prepubescent giggle fits. This is my fucking guild and we play by my fucking rules. If you so much as accidentally cast Arcane Missiles when you're supposed to cast a Fireball, I will g-fucking-kick you from this guild and make sure big brother Cachexic over here can't invite you back. Got it?"

Once again, I could tell this was Sik's way of joking around because everyone else was laughing, and in between spurts of laughter I squeezed out, "Got it."

"Good. Now shut the fuck up and don't say another word for the next four hours."

131

[Cachexic] whispers: Stick by me and you'll be fine.

[Firephunk] whispers: Ok, I will.

[Cachexic] whispers: Oh, and welcome to the guild. You'll like it here. I promise.

Chapter 7
In Fate's Hands

I had two mentors in the World of Warcraft that ultimately made me the player I became.

The first was obviously Cachexic. Our relationship quite naturally fell into the classic dichotomy between teacher and student, master and apprentice. For hours and hours, every single day, I followed him throughout the world. If he said he was doing Warsong Gulch, I joined the party and played Warsong Gulch with him. If he said he was going to camp Alliance outside of their major city, Ironforge, I made the long journey too. If he said he was going to sit outside Orgrimmar and duel other players for gold, I sat there intently and watched him duel. Every minute of every hour I spent online was with him, learning from him, watching him — as an eager oak does beside an aged oak, soaking up how to stretch for the sun.

The only times I wasn't with Cachexic was if he was part of a group I simply could not join. My gear or my skill wasn't there yet. And patiently, I would wait, training on my own with the hopes that one day I too would be an A-list player.

However, that is not to say my time spent playing with Cachexic was always "enjoyable." For the most part, it was exhausting. It was stressful and demanding. He, Revenance, and the other top players on our server with whom he socialized, accepted nothing less than perfection.

"Ok, Cole. You came to learn, so pay attention," said Cachexic.

I sat up in my chair, repositioned my headset, and placed my hands on my keyboard in the ready position. It was like sitting at a piano lesson.

"As soon as these gates open, I want you to follow me and Revenance out into midfield. If a Mage tries to sheep one of us, you Counterspell. If a Warrior looks like he's going to Charge, you Frost Nova. You have dogshit gear and you can't do dick for damage, so I expect you to be on crowd control duty."

"Got it," I said. My hands were shaking. The same thing happened before every piano recital. I could play well, I knew I could. I just got nervous under pressure.

"Let's go," said Cachexic, and off we went.

My character looked like a homeless child beside the two of them. They were celebrities, icons with the best gear in the game.

Between the two of them, they tore through the first pack of Alliance players with ease. Every time I would go to Sheep someone, Cachexic would Sheep them first. I'd try to Silence a healer, but Rev would have him Feared. Everything I tried to do was done by one of them, two full seconds before I'd even thought to do it myself.

"Firephunk, why the fuck aren't you doing anything," said Rev. His voice was calm and casual, the opposite of my internal dialogue, crazed, trying to juggle a thousand chess pieces at once.

"Yeah, Cole. What the fuck," said Cachexic.

"I'm trying!" I said, my eyes darting from corner to corner on my screen.

I saw a Rogue go into Stealth. I ran over to try to find him but Cachexic cast a Blizzard on the area and pulled him out. I tried to Sheep the Rogue, but he was already Sheeped. I turned to cast on the Warrior they were both attacking, but he died before I could get off a single Scorch. Everything was happening faster than I could react to it.

134

"COLE," yelled Cachexic.

"WHAT?" I yelled back, anxious and frustrated.

Cachexic killed the last Gnome Mage and then took a seat with Revenance. Around us were nine dead Alliance corpses.

"Hey, don't raise your fucking voice with me," said Cache. "I'm your goddamn Jedi master."

"Sorry," I said. I was afraid he'd disown me.

"I think you mean sorry, MASTER," he said.

"Sorry, Master," I said. And I was, too.

I could hear Revenance laughing in the background.

"Now, why did that second Warrior get a charge off on me?" said Cachexic.

"When?"

"There at the end. He was behind you."

"Oh, I didn't see him."

"Yeah, that much is apparent. Were you even looking?"

"I was attacking the Warlock you guys were on…"

"That's not what I asked. While that was happening, were you looking behind you?"

"No," I said, shamefully.

"And why the fuck not?"

"Because I didn't think anything was going on behind me," I said.

Rev intervened.

"A-GAME, COLE. FUCKING A-GAME."

"Listen Cole," said Cachexic. "We don't fuck around. We don't just PvP for fun. We're not some Care Bear gamers who enjoy losing. Do you understand? We PvP to be the best. So, unless you want to start paying attention, don't expect to play with us."

My stomach churned.

"Sorry," I said, practically whispering into my microphone. "I'll pay better attention next time, I promise."

"Good," said Cachexic. "Now, follow us."

For the rest of the game, and every game for months after that, I spun my camera every which way trying to stay ahead of the rhythm of battle. But still, I made mistake after mistake. They called me a faggot. They told me to get my head out of my ass. Cachexic and Revenance played on a completely different level than anyone I'd ever played with before. They saw everything. They didn't just think about what was happening right now, they thought about what was going to happen next, how it was going to happen, and what they could do to prepare for it — while still being fully engaged in the moment.

Cachexic's influence had a monumental impact on the way I saw the world.

"That's what it's all about, Cole," said Cachexic, queuing us up for another game of Warsong Gulch. "You said you wanted to learn the secret to playing a Mage? Here you go."

The secret was to play with supersonic awareness.

At a certain point, I eventually improved enough as a player that Cachexic was willing to spend more time teaching me directly, instead of just having me tag along. It was a perfectly symbiotic relationship. I was hungry to learn — the ideal apprentice, putting my full trust in Cachexic and his teachings — and Cachexic was the perfect mentor, finding great satisfaction in seeing his teachings manifest in his young pupil.

[Cachexic]: Meet me in Durotar.

136

[Firephunk]: Can't, farming gold.

[Cachexic]: I don't care. You've been gone at your brother's fucking ballerina competition all day. Meet me in Durotar.

[Firephunk]: It was a gymnastics competition. And I'm so poor. I have to farm.

[Cachexic]: No, you're not. Meet me in Durotar.

[Firephunk]: Yes I am. I still need my epic mount and I only have 55g.

[Cachexic]: Cole, an epic mount isn't going to make a fucking difference if you're still a shitty ass Mage. Now be a good Padawan and come meet me in Durotar.

[Firephunk]: Ughhhhhhhhhhh.

[Cachexic]: Oh, I'm sorry. I didn't mean to inconvenience you with my WISDOM, which is worth INFINTE TIMES MORE THAN GOLD.

Dueling each other was the equivalent of a private lesson. We had this spot off to the side, on the way to the Zepplin tower. We used duels as a way to try new strategies and perfect our playstyles.

Cachexic has defeated Firephunk in a duel.

[Cachexic]: You're still hesitating.

[Firephunk]: Yeah well maybe if we dueled less and you helped me grind Honor I'd have better gear.

[Cachexic]: You think this is about gear?

[Firephunk]: I think it plays a pretty big part.

Cachexic stripped off all his gear, his naked Undead Mage wielding only his staff.

[Firephunk]: Come on, dude. Don't do that.

137

[Cachexic]: No. I'm doing it. I want you to stop bitching about your gear because it doesn't fucking matter.

[Firephunk]: Two Fireblasts and I'll kill you. It won't even be fair.

[Cachexic]: Just duel me.

Cachexic has defeated Firephunk in a duel.

[Cachexic]: Told you.

[Firephunk]: What the fuck man. Am I seriously that bad?

[Cachexic]: No. But you seriously need to change the way you think. Gear doesn't mean shit if you don't know how to use it. Let's go again.

Cachexic has defeated Firephunk in a duel.

[Cachexic]: Again.

Cachexic has defeated Firephunk in a duel.

[Cachexic]: Again.

Cachexic has defeated Firephunk in a duel.

[Firephunk]: Dude, I can't take this anymore.

[Cachexic]: Do you want to get better or not?

[Firephunk]: Of course I do.

[Cachexic]: Then go again.

Cachexic has defeated Firephunk in a duel.

[Firephunk]: Come on, man.

[Cachexic]: Again.

[Firephunk]: No.

[Cachexic]: Hey. Don't you say no to your Jedi Master. Again.

Cachexic has defeated Firephunk in a duel.

[Firephunk]: Fuck this. I'm out.

[Cachexic]: Fine. That's enough for one day.

I would log off, furious, and show up the next day with a vengeance. Dueling Cachexic was so frustrating because the skill gap between us was astronomical. He was a superior player to me in every way. But I wanted to get better at playing a Mage more than I wanted anything else in life. So I endured loss after loss, hoping one day my practice would pay off.

What brought us together was the fact that we were both obsessed with the same goal. All we cared about was becoming the best we could be — and we took great comfort in having found another with whom we could share this pursuit.

What made it easy to stick through these very intense moments of our friendship was that, in many subtle ways, Cachexic made it clear just how important our relationship was to him. He was extremely protective. If anyone started running their mouth, calling me a terrible player, Cachexic came to my defense.

[Guild][Cachexic]: 'Scuse me. There a problem here?

[Guild][Frog]: Yeah, Firefag keeps asking to join our Warsong Gulch group and I refuse to take that cockmuncher.

[Guild][Cachexic]: I see.

[Guild][Cachexic]: Well, I can understand how you wouldn't want to take my highly trained Padawan to your little Battleground group, Frog. Would hate for him to make you look bad.

[Guild][Frog]: What did you just say to me?

[Guild][Sik]: Cache, there is no fucking chance in hell I'm

taking Firefag in our primary group. He has the worst gear in the game.

[Guild][Cachexic]: I'm calling you trash, Frog. You're in this guild because you're Sik's bitch, and the most you can hope for in this game is to let a raid boss wail on you for 20 minutes while you try to convince us all that tanking is hard.

[Guild][Fatehand]: pwned

[Guild][Sik]: Chill, Cache.

[Guild][Cachexic]: Then back the fuck up off Firephunk. He's trying to get his Honor gear. I was the one who told him to message you guys.

[Guild][Cachexic]: But it's fine. Us two will run Warsong Gulch together instead.

[Guild][Cachexic]: We'll probably win games faster anyway not having to deal with Frog carrying the flag midfield like a fucking retard.

It was an impossible dynamic to explain to anyone. Cachexic, an eighteen-year-old Persian kid from North Carolina, not only saw my potential, but was willing to spend hundreds upon hundreds of hours nurturing it. I saw him as much more than just my mentor. I looked up to him like a big brother. I told him I came from a really rich neighborhood and didn't know if I would ever become as successful as my dad, and he told me his dad was a Persian millionaire who threw money at him to make up for the fact that he'd been in and out of the picture for almost 5 years. I told him I had trouble making friends at school, and he told me that he much preferred socializing over the Internet where the only thing that mattered was how well you played the game. I told him I really wanted to lose my virginity, and he told me his dad had bought him a Persian hooker on his 16th birthday and that losing your virginity isn't all it's cracked up to be. I told him my poos took a really long time, sometimes forty-five minutes to an hour, and he told me to never use that word in his presence again, poo, because it's the

140

worst word in the English language since it sounds just like it is, and then he told me his shits took a really long time too and didn't understand how all the kids at summer camps could take a shit in five or ten minutes, and I could totally relate to that. I told him I'd been playing classical piano since I was 5, and he told me that he'd always wanted to learn how to play the piano, mostly so he could play that DJ Shadow song, *Organ Donor*. I told him that lately I'd been watching a lot of girl-on-girl porn, and he told me that girl-on-girl was a great way to change things up and that lately he'd been really into red-headed girls and blowjob scenes but it was probably just a phase. I told him I thought the best Star Wars movie was *Episode VI: Return of the Jedi*, and he said no way, the best Star Wars movie is *A New Hope* since that's where it all began. I told him my mom and I used to have a great relationship but now all we do is fight, and he said all kids go through it with their parents and it really just stems from the parents' fear of letting go. I told him that sometimes when I masturbated I would fart while I was doing it and I asked him if that was normal, and he said no that wasn't normal. I told him that today in my history class this girl in front of me was wearing this pink lace thong, and he said mmmm, lace man, lace is an unfair tool used by females to manipulate the phallus. I told him I didn't know what a phallus was, and he told me it was a penis, Cole, a phallus is a penis. I told him I was kind of worried that the first time I hooked up with a girl I wouldn't know what to do, and he told me he had some great instructional videos saved on a hard drive somewhere, he'd find them for me. I told him I really didn't even care that much about going to college, and he said that college is just one big Ponzi scheme by the government to put us all in debt and that if he could find a way to make a living playing World of Warcraft, he was going to do that.

I shared everything with Cachexic. Despite the fact that I had never seen a picture of him, didn't even know his last name for almost two years, I felt like there was someone out there who saw and accepted me, the awkward kid sitting in his computer chair. And that made all the difference.

Cachexic's influence on my life had a tremendous amount to do with the way I started to see myself as a person. He was an artist within the game, a true creative inventor whose only ambition was complete and total mastery over his character. Never had I seen someone so committed to their own development as a player — and it inherently rubbed off on me. He didn't care about raiding or collecting epic items. He didn't care about how much gold he had or how many quest rewards were collected in his bank. The only thing, and I quite literally mean the only thing, he cared about was his reputation. Not through bragging, or flaunting, or parading, but through quiet, diligent, obsessive practice. He wanted every single person to watch him in battle and, without hesitation, know him to be the greatest Mage to ever play the game.

Maybe it was because I had grown up with a silver spoon in my mouth. Maybe it was because, in my wealthy white suburb, the focus was always on the external rewards first. But I was more attracted to Cachexic's devotion to that solitary, humble goal, than I was to anything else. I didn't want his achievements. I didn't want his gear or his popularity. What I wanted was to internalize his dedication. He was monkish in his practice, devout in his focus, and because he spent thousands of hours out in the Battlefield, he moved like a God.

Cachexic has defeated Firephunk in a duel.

Cachexic has defeated Firephunk in a duel.

[Party][Firephunk]: Fucking dammit dude

[Party][Cachexic]: Again

Cachexic has defeated Firephunk in a duel.

[Party][Firephunk]: I'm going to rage

[Party][Cachexic]: You missed your Counterspell that duel. Again.

Cachexic has defeated Firephunk in a duel.

[Party][Firephunk]: Dude, why do I even bother anymore

[Party][Firephunk]: Six fucking months of this shit. I can't

142

beat you.

[Party][Cachexic]: You gonna cry?

[Party][Firephunk]: Wow, fuck you. Again.

Cachexic has defeated Firephunk in a duel.

[Party][Firephunk]: Ok, now I'm actually pissed.

[Party][Firephunk]: Brb.

I hopped on my mount and rode over to the gates of Orgrimmar where all the other players were dueling. I picked out a random Mage in full epics. His name was Sonicboom. I challenged him to a duel, and, in less than twelve seconds, he was defeated. After months of training with Cachexic, every other player paled in comparison.

Fresh off a win, I rode back to our dueling spot.

[Party][Firephunk]: There. I feel better.

[Party][Cachexic]: Hahahahaha

[Party][Cachexic]: Had to tear Sonicboom a new asshole first, eh?

[Party][Firephunk]: Wail. Yes.

[Party][Cachexic]: That's my Padawan.

Halfway through our next duel, I saw it coming. I was Bobby Fischer glimpsing twenty moves into the future. Cachexic had slipped up. He'd moved too aggressively, and now it was my turn to capitalize. He tried to Blink away and reset the fight, but it was too late. I chased him down, trapped him in a Frost Nova/Silence and wound up one final Fireball.

Firephunk has defeated Cachexic in a duel.

I wanted to explode. I wanted to yell and jump and throw my fist into the air and let everyone know that I'd finally done it!

143

The Padawan had surpassed the Master! But who in the world would understand? Could I run to my dad as I had as a child, leaping from the doors of the locker room to give him a high-five and bask in the glory of my first hockey goal? Could I find my mother in the kitchen and say in hurried, pride-filled tones, that I'd achieved the impossible? Was there a single friend at my school with whom I could share my accomplishment? Who out there in my dream so big could possibly understand the joy that rang from my core, a gong of celebration, the turning of a new leaf, the growth from boy to Mage?

Nobody. Nobody would understand. Instead, I sat in my computer chair in stillness. Cachexic didn't say a word either, our characters on the desert sand, eating and drinking back to full health and mana. Through the energy waves of the Internet, it felt as though we were right next to each other in the same room, our computers on the same desk, no barrier between us.

I'd broken through my plateau, and Cachexic had found an equal.

This marked the beginning of my rampant rise to fame, and the discovery of my own unique style as a player.

My second, and far more unlikely mentor in the World of Warcraft ended up being Sik.

At midnight on January 15th, 2007, World of Warcraft released its first expansion: *The Burning Crusade.*

In the first 24 hours, the game sold 2.4 million copies. Europe and North America, Australia and New Zealand, Singapore, Thailand, Malaysia — lines outside retail stores stretched for blocks. Gamers camped on the sidewalks in tents and sleeping bags, some dressed as Night Elves and Orcs. They shouted, "FOR THE HORDE! FOR THE ALLIANCE!" This was more than a video game. This was a Call To Arms.

Every server was packed to capacity. World of Warcraft players everywhere plopped down in their computer chairs, fingers twitching with excitement. They manically logged into the game, only to be placed in line behind thousands upon thousands of other players waiting to log in as well. Estimated wait time: 857 minutes.

Which is why if you were one of the lucky few to be allowed in game, you stayed! By God and all that is holy, you stayed. You used your vacation days and took off work. You skipped school. You did whatever you had to do, as long as it ensured that you did not leave your computer chair. You did not shower. You did not piss — that's what the empty soda bottles beside your desk were for. You did not shit unless you were one misjudged fart away from destroying your sweatpants, and even then you were expected to be back at your computer in less than two minutes. Not three. Not three and a half. Two. You did not waste time with that final wipe or the menial task of washing your hands. The only thing you were focused on was the next quest in front of you. You were aiming to be one of the first players to hit Level 70. Why? Because those would be the first players to enter the new high-end dungeons. Those players would be ahead of the gear curve and have the advantage. Those players would be the first to raid, the first to experience arenas, the first to do everything that was new. So for Level 70, you did not sleep. For Level 70, you did not eat anything requiring a cooking time that exceeded 38 seconds. For Level 70, you sat in front of your computer and pushed yourself to grind until it was 4:30 in the morning and your eyeballs felt like lead weights on a fishing line pulling your bobbing head down toward your desk, face first. Only then did you allow yourself to go to bed, but not before setting your alarm for 6:30 a.m., a two hour interim, two hours of sleep was plenty, that way you'd be back up and in your desk chair before the morning rush of players and there would be no wait time, no long line to enter your server. You'd log online bright and early, see your entire guild do the same

——

[Guild][Revenance]: Wail, looks like it's Skittles and a warm can of iced tea for breakfast

— and you'd spend the entire day doing as you did the day before. Not stopping. Unrelenting. Until you reached Level 70.

That's what an MMORPG expansion launch is like. It's beautiful in its discipline, manic in its commitment.

It's what I should have been doing.

Instead, I was sitting in Room 13B taking a History final.

[Mrs. Mayer]: "You have 3 hours to complete the exam. Good luck."

I flipped through the thick packet. I tapped my pencil on my desk. The first twenty pages were all multiple choice. I had conspiracy theories about this kind of testing. I analyzed the pattern my answers took: A, A, B, C, B, B, B, B. Four B's in a row. I had to be wrong — I had to be. No teacher would make four straight questions have B answers.

Tired, so tired from staying up anticipating midnight's expansion launch and annoyed with a test designed to make me feel stupid, I flipped to the back where I found a couple essay questions.

Explain the Boston Tea Party.

Who started the First World War?

What was the Cuban Missile Crisis?

I answered with conviction: "The Cuban missile crisis was a crisis in which the Cubans, who were very much a part of this, had missiles, and many others had missiles as well, and this was not very good for anyone and so it became a crisis, thus, the Cuban missile crisis."

I just wanted to get out of there. The classroom was no place for a boy like me.

As soon as I turned in my exam, I ran outside to call Lidia to come pick me up. Both my parents were at work for the rest of the day, which meant I was free to explore the new World of Warcraft expansion.

Like a tornado, I rampaged the kitchen to stock up on

146

provisions: Doritos (wheat), Lidia's special lemon sponge cake (wheat), pretzels (wheat), orange juice, and a bag of turkey lunchmeat. As soon as I got to my room, I unloaded my haul on my desk. I took off my shirt, took off my jeans, and replaced them with sweatpants and a Nike T-shirt. I grabbed a pillow from my bed and put it on top of my footstool, under my desk. I draped a blanket over the back of my desk chair, able to be folded over my shoulders in case I got cold. I turned on my computer and while the operating system started up I ran to the bathroom one last time before committing to a few hours of disciplined grinding. My mom usually got home at 6:00 p.m., so I was safe until about 5:55 p.m.

Or so I thought.

I positioned my headset over my ears. Sik had formed a new guild, <Loot Crusade>, on the server Black Dragonflight. Cachexic and I had transferred (again) to join him. A new expansion and another server transfer gave me the opportunity to recreate myself one last time. The name Firephunk was a younger me. A less experienced me. I was older now, stronger, and ready to step into my best self.

My name was Exitec.

Mouth full of Doritos and sliced turkey, I said, "Sup guys!"

"I knew my day was going to get worse," said Sik.

"Hi Cole," said Cachexic.

"HAY PHUNKY FIRE," yelled Rev.

"Fucking Firefag is in the new guild?" said Frog.

"My name is Exitec now," I said with pride, hoping at some point it would catch on.

"It was a package deal. He came with Cachexic," said Sik.

"Any way we can send the homosexual part of the package back?" said Frog.

147

"How's the expansion?" I asked. I typed my password into the login screen and was placed in queue. Position: 1,442. Estimated wait time: 279 minutes. The expansion launch had turned out to be so much bigger than anyone had anticipated.

"It's incredible and you're missing out," said Sik.

"A lot has changed, and Rogues are huge cock-munchers now, but pretty cool overall," said Cachexic.

"HUGE CAWK-MUHNCHERS," yelled Revenance.

"How long did you guys have to wait to get in?" I asked. My position in queue wasn't moving.

"Well, unlike you, Firefag, some of us prioritized bettering ourselves in the World of Warcraft and were up at the crack of dawn chugging Red Bull so we wouldn't have to wait," said Sik.

"Yeah Cole, what the fuck," said Cache.

"I had finals," I said.

"That sucks limp donkey penis," said Revenance.

"Revenance FUCKING HEAL ME," yelled Sik.

"I'M SHADOW SPECCED, I'M NOT HEALING YOU," yelled Revenance.

"IF YOU LET ME DIE I WILL SEND YOU ANTHRAX IN THE FUCKING MAIL."

"FINE, HERE'S A SHIELD."

"Rev and Sik are a little tired," said Cachexic. The rest of the guild laughed.

And while I waited in line to be let into the game, I really should have been studying for the massive Chemistry exam I had the next day. But I didn't. I couldn't! I was much too excited. Instead, I read the WoW forums and listened to the guild talk about the new quests, the new zones, which porn star they thought could

148

execute the perfect blowjob (the consensus was Jenna Jameson), etc.

Sik's new guild was the best of the best, made especially for the new expansion. There were only 71 people in the guild — 40 core raiders, 15 alternates, 15 material gatherers — people whose only interests were to stock up on materials for the guild bank — and then me.

By the time I got into the World of Warcraft, it was 5:15 p.m. I'd waited almost two hours.

Except, low and behold, my mother must have had a student cancel on her, because at 5:30 p.m. she silently pulled into the driveway. She nudged open the door to my bedroom, and since my headphones muffled my ears and the entire guild was laughing in my headset, I'm quite positive she stood there and watched me for quite some time without me knowing. Watched how my body was stuck in an L shape, my legs straight out under my desk resting on my footstool and pillow, my upper body erect. Watched how my head never once turned right or left. Watched how my eyes darted around the screen like a crazed dreamer. Watched how my hands seemed separate from the rest of my body, my right hand clicking click click click click click, my left hand tapping tap tap tap tap tap tap. Watched how I would haphazardly claw at my pile of food, shoveling Doritos (wheat) and slices of turkey toward my face in one swift and sloppy motion. Watched the crumbs make an anthill on my sweatpants. Watched the orange juice dribble down my chin. Watched me wipe my mouth with the inside of my shirt collar. She might have even, if her eyes were detective enough (which I'm sure they were), watched me fart and suddenly clench in terror, the tide turning against me, a river of wet worry probing to be let loose, while at the same time observing my refusal to depart for the bathroom and grant myself that privilege, witnessing my relentless dedication to my desk chair, my current position, the World of Warcraft.

"Cole!" she said louder, and I quickly jolted in my chair. I ripped my headphones off and turned toward her. My heart rate skyrocketed. I wondered how long she'd been standing in my

149

doorway.

"Mom? Hey. You're home early."

"What are you doing?" she said, giving me a look of fury. I tried my best to salvage the situation.

"Oh, I just had to check something real quick," I said.

Tactic: Downplay the situation.

"Cole, we explicitly told you there would be no playing on your computer during finals week."

Tactic: Deflection.

"No, I know. I wasn't, Mom. I swear. I was just sending my friend an item, he needed an item I had."

Behind me, my Undead Mage was slowly dying to a boar, little red numbers popping up on my screen.

"Cole, that's not the point. You should be studying for your exams."

Tactic: Offensive attack.

"Mom, seriously, I wasn't playing, I was doing my friend a favor. I stopped studying for literally 3 minutes. I'm about to go right back to studying. I don't understand why you're freaking out."

She reloaded her eyes and fired her eyebrows high.

"You think this is me freaking out?"

"I think you're getting upset over nothing."

"So prioritizing Warcraft World over your final exams is something I should just be ok with?" she said, crossing her arms.

"First of all, it's World of Warcraft. And second..."

She cut me off, her bright blonde hair swaying like a guillotine as she shook her head in disappointment.

150

"You know what, Cole? This is exactly why your father and I have been so frustrated lately. You can't even have a conversation without getting upset."

"I'm not getting upset!"

"You're yelling right now!"

"NO I'M NOT."

My mother, a much more advanced player than me, suddenly took a step back, laughing lightly, so soft and playful, the most terrifying laugh. It was as if she were telling me in a whisper the very ground upon which my life was built was about to cave in.

With a smile she said, "No, Cole. You're not yelling at all."

Her voice was like velvet — the clothes of the emperor moments before the beheading.

I scrambled for my life.

Tactic: Retreat.

"Mom, look. I'm sorry, ok? I'm really stressed out because of finals. I just want you to believe me. I wasn't playing World of Warcraft, I just had to log on for two seconds."

On my computer screen, the boar took the last of my health. My Mage fell dead.

"Ok," she said, using her wispy and nightmarish voice. "I believe you."

"Mom!" I yelled.

"No, it's fine," she said, and slowly closed the door.

Not three minutes after my father pulled into the driveway that night, he went right back out to his BMW and drove to the local hardware store — per my mother's orders. He bought an industrial grade lockbox with a combination lock, came home, and grabbed a power drill off the garage wall. He drilled a hole in the

151

side of the lockbox, and then went into the basement and jailed the modem, running the Ethernet and power chords through the hole before snapping the combination lock shut.

His son? Playing World of Warcraft during finals week?

Not in this family.

"Dad, please!" I yelled, running after him up the basement stairs to the kitchen. The Internet was off and there was nothing I could do about it.

"Maybe this will teach you to obey our rules," he said, calmly picking up his late plate from the marble counter and sitting down at the sunroom table.

But was I so easily defeated?

That night, after the house had fallen into sleep, I tiptoed downstairs to the modem's newly made jail cell. I found a flashlight from the storage closet and peered into the hole my father had drilled into the side of the lockbox. There, I saw the unthinkable. He'd connected a timer to the router, with the dial set to 7:00 a.m and 3:00 p.m. Between those hours, the Internet would be alive — the hours I was at school. Once 3:00 p.m struck, it would fall dead.

I sat on the white carpet of our downstairs office with the lockbox, coaxing it, speaking with it, asking its prerogative. "I will conquer you," I whispered, running my fingers along its sharp edges. When my fingers reached the combination lock, I fondled the dial, spinning it slowly. I got down on my stomach and pressed my ear close as I turned it. I was listening for a click. I'd seen this done in a movie.

When it became clear that the legs of the lock would not be pulled open with any brute force, I resorted to more seductive measures. I stuck my pointer finger through the hole, tickling the inside wires. When such teasing proved infantile, I grabbed a pair of scissors from my father's oak desk drawer and tried cutting the hole bigger, clipping away at the coarse plastic, leaving violent scratch marks. When the hole refused to widen, I came to the

152

conclusion that there was only one way I would be granted access. I had to pry the edge of the lockbox open just enough to slip my hand in and flip the timer.

I grabbed the corner of the lid and the base and pulled them apart as hard as I could. The industrial-grade plastic sliced at my tender fingers, stinging them, turning them bright red. I let go and the lid snapped shut.

There was no way I'd be able to hold the lid open long enough. I would have to let it close on my wrist while my fingers worked blindly inside. I prepared myself for the excruciating pain.

Again, I pulled the corner of the lid as hard as I could, opening the lockbox barely an inch, just enough to sneak my bony hand in. The lid came down on my wrist, crushing it like a pair of jaws. I was lucky my hand wasn't severed clean off my arm.

Once my fingers were inside, I searched around for the modem. I walked my fingertips to the back and felt for the Ethernet chord. When I found the wire, I followed it a few inches until I reached a round device with a notched wheel on the front. This was the timer.

I spun the dial 180 degrees, hearing the clicks of the notches as it turned.

When I finally pulled my hand out, I examined my wrist. It had been chewed by the edge. There were cuts and scratches right above my palm. I very well could have sliced a vein — an accidental suicide. But I had won, and that's all that mattered.

I tiptoed back upstairs to my bedroom and checked my computer. The Internet was alive! I had to wait in the queue to enter the game again, but once I was in, I played World of Warcraft for about an hour, exploring the new expansion, finally getting to experience the quests and the brand new Outland continent. When the clock struck 1:00 a.m., I ran downstairs and stuck my hand back in the lockbox, turning the dial 180 degrees again. The Internet vanished.

For the entire week of final exams, this, ladies and gentlemen, is how I continued to play World of Warcraft right beneath my parents' noses.

The next day, I told the guild what had happened: the lockbox, my parents, and why I was the only person in the guild who hadn't gained a single level since the new expansion's release.

"You see? That's the type of shitty parenting I'm talking about," said Sik. He was already a bottle of wine deep. He was slurring his words.

"Sik, you would be a terrible parent," said Rev.

"I WOULD BE AN INCREDIBLE FATHER," Sik yelled.

All of a sudden, we heard Sik's girlfriend walk in the door behind him. His voice over Ventrilo went soft.

"Hey baby. Yup, just getting ready for tonight's raid. No, it's alright, you can eat without me. How was work baby? Good? Hey, can you make me a sandwich?"

We listened closely, peering into Sik's personal life.

He continued: "You're tired? I told you I can't right now, I'm getting ready to lead the raid. No, not now. Later. I'm hungry. Please? Crystal. Crystal I said make me a god damn sandwich. Yes, there's wine in the kitchen. No, I drank all the red. I left the white for you because I'm not a pussy."

There was a thudding sound as Sik repositioned his headset over his head. "Sorry guys, my girlfriend is being a dumb whore. What did I miss?"

"Sik, if I was your girlfriend I'd slap the shit out of you," said Hippykillers, the only woman in our guild and the Druid class leader.

"And that's exactly why I would never sleep with your smelly cunt," said Sik.

154

Ventrilo burst into laughter. This was the guild's sense of humor.

"Hey Firefag," said Sik. "You ever been drunk before?"

I had no interest in drinking alcohol.

"No, never," I said.

"Maybe if your parents saw you get fucked up like all the other teenagers out there, they'd let you play on your fucking computer more. I know your dad has a liquor cabinet, you need to go raid that shit and show him how much worse things could be for you."

"Eh," I said. That sounded like a terrible idea.

"No, don't EH me. You don't know shit about the world. I assume you're a virgin too?"

I didn't answer. My silence spoke for me.

"Oh my God. Ok. Listen, Firefag. Monday. When you show up to your shitty ass high school in your stupid ass Abercrombie shirt, I want you to find five candidates and bring them back to me for assessment. We are going to find you a slut."

"I don't think…" I said, trying to defend myself. The whole guild was listening.

"I want names and pictures. I don't care how you do it. Camera phone, whatever. Then, after we've found which slut will be taking your tiny penis in her gaping vagina, we will find you some pot and really get the ball rolling."

"Sik, we're trying to help the kid, not ruin his life," said Cachexic. He was cut off by Sik's screaming.

"NO CRYSTAL, SHUT THE FUCK UP, CAN'T YOU SEE I'M HAVING A VERY SERIOUS CONVERSATION WITH FIREFAG OVER HERE?"

155

Crystal started sobbing in the background. Sik's cat was meowing loudly. We could hear Sik guzzling down the rest of his bottle.

"Firefag, whatever you do, don't date a girl for her boobs. Ok? Because then you'll end up with THIS kind of shitbasket. YES CRYSTAL, I'M CALLING YOU A DIRTY HOOKER OVER THE INTERNET. NEXT TIME MAKE ME A GOD DAMN SANDWICH."

Meanwhile, the rest of the raid group was preparing for their first attempt at one of the new raid dungeons: Gruul's Lair.

"Firefag, you listen to me, and you listen good, ya hear?" said Sik.

Rev took this opportunity to chime in with his southern redneck voice.

"NA YEW LISTEN HERE AND YEW LISTEN GUUD."

"Rev, shut the fuck up," said Sik.

"'Scuse yew."

"Firefag, I know you're not going to believe me, and that's alright, I'll have my laughs about it later, but let me explain something to you. Contrary to what your parents or the rest of society might tell you about being responsible, it's all bullshit. You need to get some real life experience and you need to get it fast. Do you know what happens to kids like you? Never getting drunk, never banging sluts, having their parents controlling their every move? They leave for college and suddenly there aren't any rules and they don't know what to do with themselves. There was a girl from my town who was like that. The nicest little Catholic schoolgirl you've ever met. And do you know what happened the first week she went off to college? She had to call her dad. Because she had herpes. Because she thought it would be a good idea to take two dicks at the same time, one up the butthole and one up the vagina. Do you want to be that little Catholic schoolgirl, Firefag?

156

Do you?"

"Jesus, Sik," said Cachexic, laughing.

"I could see Kowle being a very kewte kewte Catholic skewlgirl," said Rev.

"Pretty sure that's not going to happen," I said.

"I promise you, Firefag, you're going to rebel," said Sik. "You've been rebelling this whole time. Now imagine what's going to happen when your parents aren't there to stop you."

Ventrilo went quiet and Sik's words rang out.

"You're going to rebel and it's going to be fantastic. So you might as well start now while you have us here to supervise."

I thought Sik had lost his mind.

So I'm sure you're wondering what on earth I mean when I say that Sik ended up being a mentor to me — and truthfully, not just a mentor, but one of the most influential people in my entire life.

The way Sik ran his guild was extremely detailed. He expected every one of his core raiders to be online fifteen minutes before each raid, no questions asked. If you were late, you were replaced. If you were late twice, you were kicked out of the guild. Every few days, there would be guild meetings for 30 minutes. Every member was expected to show up. If you were late, you were not allowed in the Ventrilo channel, and you were made to do something embarrassing like post a picture of yourself on the guild forums for all to ridicule in a way that would make any gym class trash talk seem like candlelight dinner conversation. Guild meetings were transcribed — usually by an initiate or someone lowly, like myself. The transcription was dated and posted on the forums immediately following the guild meeting. If you missed more than two guild meetings in a month, you were kicked. When Sik opened the floor during each guild meeting for members to voice their concerns or qualms with other players, if you did not address them out in the open like a mature adult, you were kicked. If you did not contribute a certain amount of gold or materials to the guild bank for the core raid group each week, you were suspended from all guild activities that week. If you did not contribute for two weeks in a row, you were kicked. If you made a big, big mistake during a raid, you were screamed at by Sik in a way that would make you wish you were never born. And if you made the same big, big mistake twice, you were kicked, and then Sik or an Officer would post, with screenshots, all over the World of Warcraft forums about what a terrible player you were, ensuring your name got blacklisted by every top guild on the server.

Being in <Loot Crusade> was like being in the army.

That said…There were a lot of things Sik didn't care about. If you wanted to trash talk other players in Orgrimmar all day, you could. If you wanted to pull pranks on other guilds, hop into their Ventrilo channels and pretend to be a horny eighteen-year-old schoolgirl, Sik would usually accompany you in hopes of self-entertainment. If you wanted to start a war on the forums, you were allowed to — whereas other guilds, especially the competitive ones, had very strict rules against starting drama. But for Sik, what players did on their own time, even with the <Loot Crusade> name attached to their backs, didn't matter. If anything, he encouraged each player's individuality. And it was this blend between structured discipline that drove results, and an unstructured freedom to play the game however you wanted, that instilled an unbreakable bond of loyalty throughout the guild.

The truth is, Sik was an average player, at best. In the new expansion, he played a Priest, and he was not one of the best Priests on the server. He was good. He was consistent. But he was nowhere near the level of someone like Revenance, for example. Sik's value was that he was a leader. He knew how to manage people's personalities so well, that every single member of that guild would have stayed up for three days straight if Sik had asked it of them. He knew how to teach, inspire, and get the best out of each and every member — even if that meant deploying unconventional ways of doing so.

158

Although I was not a core raider, Sik let me tag around. He made fun of me, he called me names, he thought my family was Mormon and joked that I would be a virgin for the rest of my life, but through it all, he made me a better player.

What I learned from Sik was very different than what I learned from Cachexic. Cachexic was a master craftsman, and I was his apprentice, mimicking and parodying his distinct style until I became fluent enough to develop my own. But Sik is the one who taught me, even just by allowing me to watch, how to put my ego aside for the betterment of the group. With him, it was always about the collective, the guild, its whole being stronger than the sum of its parts. <Loot Crusade> was such a rare group of individuals. There was no closer guild out there, period. And the guild did not succeed because each member was filled with talent. If anything, its members were exceedingly average, when judged on their own merit. But together, the guild was an unstoppable force. Sik had found a way to create an environment that brought the best out of everyone, and as a result, made a championship winning team out of mostly B-list players.

I still consider my time in <Loot Crusade> to be one of my most formative life experiences.

Obviously, my parents did not agree.

It really was a joke in our guild how much I had to navigate the rules of my parents — the faking going to sleep, the tiptoeing back to my computer in the middle of the night. And I have often wondered (and to this day, wonder) why my parents didn't just pull the plug on my little rodeo. They had that power. Freshman year, after my back had healed. Sophomore year, when purple bags began to appear under my eyes. Junior year, preparing for the ACT, filling out college applications — they very well could have kidnapped my desktop in the middle of the night and held it ransom, demanded an arm and a leg, celibacy until marriage, the promise to become a reverend; all petty prices I would have paid for one more afternoon with my computer. But they didn't. Instead, they instituted reading lists and a rigorous allowance system, longer family dinners, more family movie nights, demanded that I sit, sit Cole, enjoy this time with your family, unless, unless you'd rather be doing something else? I would force a Cheshire smile and shake my head no, no mother, wouldn't miss another nightly viewing of *Mary Poppins* for the world! She would smile back, lips coated in passive-aggressive pleasure:

[Mom]: "Good. We're so happy you're with us."

It was as if they wanted this silent war to rage on.

And I know what you're thinking. Cole, that's not so much to ask, is it? A little time with your family? A little, shall we say, *balance?* To which I would agree, no, not much to ask at all! Except for the fact that if I were asking to be excused from the dinner table to attend another long rehearsal for the speech team state finals this weekend, needing to spend the rest of the night drilling home my monologues (there would be no time for homework), my mother would have halted our very earth's revolutions to get me to that rehearsal, would have begged to stick around and watch from the rafters, "I promise you won't even know I'm there!" Or had I asked, "Excuse me Father, but would you mind if I left the table early to go study for medical school? I know I'm only sixteen but, you know how it is, that itch; all I want to do is learn!" I cannot express to you the intensity with which my father would have taken one last sip of his brandy and pointed at me from across the table to reveal to the rest of our clan that I was the standard to which the rest of my siblings should aim; they should be more like me. Cole here is putting in the work that will one day yield greatness.

But if I were to politely bring up, so politely, as if requesting they please pass the green beans, "Excuse me? Mother? Father? Wouldest thou mind if raideth I do, this fortnight?" The horror! Raiding? On a Tuesday? You must be out of your mind!

"So let me get this straight," Cachexic said. I sat in my computer chair with my head in my hands, my headset over my ears. My parents had just received my junior year first semester grades in the mail. I had straight C's.

160

"Your parents want to send you to a therapist because you spend your free time playing a video game instead of being like every other robotic adolescent and joining some shitty-ass after-school club? Am I getting this right?"

"Yes," I said, my voice defeated. My life was over. They would — this time they would — make me quit the game. Everything I had worked so hard for, gone.

"Is this a joke? Are you trolling me right now? Because if you're being serious then I think your parents are the ones who need to go see a therapist. Don't you get like straight A's and shit too?"

"Eh, mostly C's."

"What the fuck, dude. If I got those grades my mom would be ecstatic."

"Yeah well, that's considered failing in my family."

"Have you met this therapist yet? Is he one of those 'I'm going to agree with everything your parents say so that I can charge $500 an hour' kind of guys?"

"I'm not sure. Apparently I'm seeing him in 45 minutes."

"Let's hope he's not. Otherwise, you're fucked."

"Thanks."

"But! But. If he's cool, then maybe he'll actually listen to you and tell your parents they're overbearing as shit."

A pause.

"This could be really good actually," Cache said. "Maybe if they hear it from someone with a fancy title in front of their name, things might change."

"Heh. Maybe."

"Hey, I'm trying to be supportive here. Quit being a Debbie

161

fucking Downer."

"Sorry, I'm just really upset."

"I would be too. But I'll tell you this. I'm going to be SUPER fucking pissed if my Padawan can't play WoW anymore because he fucked it up with some therapist. Get your head in the game and get him on your side."

"I don't think that's possible."

"Cole. Anything is possible. Remember? The first step in becoming a Master is BELIEVING that you're a Master."

An hour later, my mother and I were following a portly man down a narrow hallway. His name was Dr. Sylis. His office was decorated with diplomas on the walls and books in big, wooden bookshelves. Against the back wall was a long, leather couch, and opposite it, a chair with a high back. Dr. Sylis took his seat, crossed both legs, and motioned for us to take our places on the couch.

I sat on one end; my mother sat on the other.

She began immediately.

[Mom]: "Dr. Sylis, I want to thank you for seeing us on such short notice. I'll be the first to admit that this hasn't been easy for any of us. Especially Cole. He was very apprehensive about coming today. I would just like to say before we begin that both his father and I reached out to you only because we love our son and want nothing more than to see him succeed."

[Dr. Sylis]: "And where is his father today?"

[Mom]: "Oh, he couldn't make it. He is a spine surgeon, I'm not sure if I told you that. He's very busy. But as I was saying, I feel like I've watched Cole continue to spiral for a while now, and I don't think any of us should be ashamed to admit that maybe he needs a little extra help."

My arms were crossed and my eyes were on the window. I didn't bother arguing with her. She couldn't hear me.

162

Dr. Sylis took note of my unconcerned gaze and cut my mother short.

[Dr. Sylis]: "Would you mind if I spoke to Cole alone?"

[Mom]: "Not at all! In fact, I think that might be just what he needs."

She patted my shoulder twice with her fingertips, *there there*, grabbed her white purse and left the room.

I kept my gaze on the window and the tree just outside it. I would wait the hour out if I had to.

[Dr. Sylis]: "Cole, I want you to know that this is an open space."

I mumbled something. Uh huh.

[Dr. Sylis]: "Anything you say here is just between you and me."

I turned to look at him. His hair was patted down to the top of his balding head — a toupee? He was chewing the end of his pen. I did not like him.

[Me]: "What do you want me to say?"

[Dr. Sylis]: "Anything you'd like."

[Me]: "So then you can tell my mom?"

[Dr. Sylis]: "I am legally obligated to keep anything you tell me private. Unless you mention thoughts of harming yourself or another human being. Otherwise, it's just between you, me, and the lamp."

I looked at the lamp.

[Me]: "Really?"

[Dr. Sylis]: "Really."

I scratched behind my ear.

[Me]: "Well, in that case…"

Chapter 8
Just Lose It

My parents? Heh. I really shouldn't. That's one of those doors I'm not supposed to open, even to you. I'm sure you can understand the sort of trouble I'd get in for exposing them. Not that they did anything wrong! Please don't get the wrong idea. I'm not here to defame them — that's not my intention. The only thing I ever wished for was to be heard.

Let's just say things are better than they used to be. I couldn't see it as a teenager, but they really did care about me. They just wanted me to succeed. The trouble is — and I'm trusting you'll keep this between you and me — is I feel I never got to tell my side of the story. They'll claim otherwise; believe me, whenever I go spouting off my feelings to the world, they're the first to yell libel. But why do they think it's always about them? Just because I feel or experience something and I want to talk about it doesn't mean I'm out to ruin their reputation. That was their biggest fear when I made the mistake of mentioning to them my undertaking this memoir. Not my brightest idea, I'll admit, to expect support from the antagonists themselves. They were worried I'd go on some terrible rant for 348 pages about what terrible parents they are; that I'd make them out to be the bad guys. If I'm being honest, the first draft I wrote wasn't fair to them. I was still very, very angry.

I discovered the material while studying Creative Writing at Columbia College Chicago. I was taking a Journal and Sketchbook class taught by an author herself, Patty McNair — one of my favorite teachers, truly. And how fitting, because did you know I got my start writing in a journal? I did! I can't say I was ever one of those aspiring novelists stacking short stories and rejection letters on my desk, chasing the dream of linguistic wealth. The closest I ever got to that Moveable Feast was in a journal I kept on my dad's laptop, which I brought in with me to the toilet. I treated every saved page of Microsoft Word as though my journal would one day be published as the documentation of a bathroom philosopher, detailing quite insightfully my perspectives on the very world I did not have the freedom to roam and explore. I would email the documents to myself at the end of each bowel movement, and then the delete the files and empty the trash as not to be seen ever by my father's eyes. It worked well for me.

Anyways, in this Journal and Sketchbook class, Patty prompted us to write about our adolescence. And one of my World of Warcraft stories just came right out. Plop. Right there on the page. I didn't know what to do with it. I'd never written about my years playing video games, never much elaborated on it in my journals outside of teenage ramblings against authority. But there it was in all its vulnerability. It was a very early version of what would later become the *Make Them Hear You* chapter. I had to read it aloud in class.

And ahhh, the anxiety! Keep in mind, these were not very judgmental people — my classmates. They had purple hair and nose rings and carried animé comic books in their hipster satchels strung from left shoulder to right hip, if that's any testament to my own insecurities. It was an art school, and common for my fashionably dressed male peers to write about the first time they were plunged in the anus by a blonde-haired Bobby on a cozy Christmas night; where girls spoke freely of their eating disorders and scarred wrists; and here I was, terrified to the core to sing of such a day when I, the kid in the Adidas sweatpants, was once a Gladiator in the World of Warcraft.

Well, Patty thought my story was great. She was the one who pushed me to continue exploring the material. "The Material." Such a great way of giving the soul appropriate distance to explore by calling it "The Material." And distance did I need.

So much so, that I wrote the entire first draft of this memoir in the third person. Now, maybe you're not a writer, and that's all right, but let me explain: Nobody writes a memoir in the third person. 'Cole did this, Cole did that.' I'm Cole! Why not just say 'I!' I'll tell you. I'll tell you because I trust that you'll keep this a secret. One of my biggest fears in life is to be misunderstood. I know it's very particular, but it's true. 'I' simply felt too wild, too uncontrollable. No, I needed everything to be perfect, and none of it could be directly aimed at my parents — an impossible request no matter my approach, I know now. My belief was that by writing in the third person, I would be able to detach myself from the emotional component that would inevitably get me in trouble with the dictators themselves — the unlimited bank account that was still paying my college tuition, my room and board, my monthly stipend of food, and my sense of identity in this economical world of wealth-based humanity.

Thus, the main character was not I — he was Cole.

And is this not the theme of my life? This constant search of self? Let me go off on a tangent for moment, if you don't mind, because this is simply too good a connection to ignore. Do you know my real name isn't even Cole? It's Nicolas. That's what's on my birth certificate. Now, have I ever been called Nicolas? Has an overprotective mother or disappointed father ever lost temper and made the switch from familiar to formal? Never. Not ever.

And why? Why, oh why, must I live with this false name? Unfortunately, I have an answer. It was my father's idea (although my mother agreed, let us not forget that). "I like Cole, but Cole isn't good enough," he said, holding my newborn space suit in his arms, ready to give it a name. "He needs a strong name. A respectable name. In case he ever becomes something important, like a lawyer or a doctor. Nicolas! Now that should be his real name! Not Cole."

THE IRONY! Yes, let's name our son one thing, and let's have that thing symbolize success in the utmost, but then let's call him by another. Down the middle, he will be split. This is who you are, and this is who you should be. Who you should be, we will never call you — Nicolas. And who you are, which isn't good enough, shall be your name — Cole. Christ. I was doomed from the start.

That is why I have decided to put all of my art under the name Nicolas Cole. Through expression, I hope to make amends within myself and merge the two.

But back to what I was saying: I wrote the first draft of this book, the whole thing, in the third person. Quite avant-garde for a memoir, wouldn't you say? And I thought everything was going swimmingly, what with my unique form and all. Actually, I took it a step further and wrote half the book, the real-life chapters, in third person and the other half, the chapters where I wrote from the perspective of a young Mage in the World of Warcraft, in first person — my Mage self "I" being something more manageable. I wanted to draw further emphasis to how much I had distanced myself from my peers and family to live a life primarily online. I still find that draft brilliant. Most especially in its naivety.

But so it goes. My junior year of college, my parents, the first to support me in all my socially acceptable endeavors, funded my studying abroad. Prague and Italy for the whole summer — does a child get any luckier? I was taking creative writing classes, per my major, but spent the majority of my time working on my book. For 10 weeks I did nothing but read and write, read and write, nostalgically barreling through my adolescence like a madman. It was not uncommon for me to write eight hours in a day. I couldn't type fast enough! Though, can you not see the shadow of guilt I carried? Here I was, biting the hand that was feeding me, spending my free summer in another country to write — "Our son, the next Hemingway!" — about the very issues that have crippled and long strained the relationship I have with my parents. This theme of being given everything and yet made to feel guilty for it is one only us privileged can understand. And just like everything else in our well-funded lives, it is swept under the rug and suppressed from ever rising to the surface.

Well, wouldn't you believe it. My grandma — Dad's mom — emailed me Happy Birthday while I was away, and I emailed her back Thank You, as any upstanding grandson would do. Except in my email signature was a link to a travel blog I'd been keeping online, which she, apparently interested, decided to click. And on what day did she embark on such a digital exploration? The day we visited a sex shop in Prague! If you didn't know, sex is viewed very differently in other countries. Here in America, it's taboo. We don't talk about sex. We sell sex, we love sex, but we don't talk about it — sort of like how we treat wealth: the goal of the masses, its horrors undisclosed. And as a twenty-two year old tourist in a foreign country, I found this fascinating. I mean come on, a sex shop on the same street as an elementary school? That's different! So I wrote about it. And Grandma was disgusted.

Grandma called Dad. Dad yanked my bank account. This was nothing new, being fined by the ruling government. Here I was, overseas, with him threatening to pull funding from the rest of my trip unless I delete the blog immediately — my father of course assuming this one single blog post on the Internet is being seen right now, right this second, by every pair of eyeballs multiplied by the size of humanity. I mean really, what was I going to do? Walk down to the embassy, pick up a work visa, and between classes bag groceries at the local mart in the name of free speech? Whatever. I deleted it. Not just that post, the entire blog. That was the least discouraging part. What hurt worse was the sudden realization that if this impromptu objective essay about global sexuality had warranted such aggressive action, then God could only guess the hellfire that awaited the publishing of my book.

It should come as no surprise that I immediately stopped writing. Not by choice, but by despair. I walked the streets of Prague lost in its dreamy architecture, arguing endlessly with the internalized parental figures in my head about how at some point they had to let go. I am who I am. I'm going to do things in life they won't necessarily agree with. But just like how, when they do things that I don't agree with either, I don't threaten them. I don't say, "Believe what I believe, or I won't be your son anymore!" I did a lot of journaling for the rest of that trip, trying to come to terms, again, with their expectations of me. I didn't pick my story back up until my final weeks in Italy.

When I returned to the states, my next teacher — this was

my senior year of college — taught a class entirely focused around writing about those things that scare us. "The goldmine," he called it, and hesitant was I to show him mine. I believe they call it Post Traumatic Stress Disorder. PTSD. I tried writing about some other things instead, silly stories, poop stories, but one girl wrote about losing her virginity, and this guy who always wore deep colors and rugged leather and just looked like he was bound to become a successful author wrote about when he was younger and his older brother had left for the military, and this very genuine part of me jumped out because I knew I had a story worth sharing. The girl and her virginity, the boy and his older brother, those stories were relatable, sure, don't get me wrong, but they didn't do a very good job with the telling. Too much tiptoeing around the subject — "*she glared, he imagined.*" Come on! Tell us how you felt! Rage war! Give us blood!

The next week, I turned in probably twenty chapters of pure World of Warcraft, convinced that my teacher would give me the validation I was seeking. Not so. He handed back my memoir-in-progress unmarked, and when I approached him after class he quite directly told me to grow a pair of balls. I really liked him as a professor. Not then, obviously, but much later. He was right. He said memoirs are written in the first person for a reason, and it's to hear the heartbeat of the author. The very things I criticized in my classmates writing — a lack of emotional depth, to be specific — was the dead root in my own tree of loose leaf.

It took me weeks to approach the material again. "The Material." Weeks. Here I had written just about the entire book, only for my teacher to, essentially, tell me to start over. A year and a half of work, poof. Gone. I contemplated burning it. I sat at my laptop, an empty page, and watched the cursor blink, blink. When I would find a pinch of courage, I'd begin to write. And then as soon as that dreadful letter appeared, "I," both my shoulders went heavy and on the right was my father and on the left was my mother and they convinced me it wasn't worth writing. Nobody wants to hear your story, Cole. Maybe someone else's, but not yours. We didn't let you play your little video game — poor you. Are you really that ungrateful? Have you not seen all that we have given you? Do you know how many children in the world would give all their fingers and toes for a family like yours? All you do is complain. "Look what you made me do." That's what people who can't take accountability say. And how will that reflect on us? Not good. There's no guidebook for parenting, you know that, right?

I showed up in Patty McNair's office, heartbroken. She was the Department Chair. I said, "There's no handbook for dealing with your parents either!" I told her if I wrote from the heart they'd kick me out of the family. How my parents would never speak to me again. She chuckled and refused to believe they would do such a thing. I did not laugh back. I told her no, you don't understand. They will. They've done it before.

She pointed me to the greats. "Dostoevsky wrote the first version of *Crime and Punishment* in first person, only to realize it needed to be in third. And he actually burned his first draft!" she said. That was a nice ego boost. I'll admit it. Twenty-two years old and on par with the great Russian linguist.

I bought every book I could find about the process of writing. *On Writing* by Stephen King. *Bird by Bird* by Anne Lamott. Somewhere out there was an answer on how to navigate the waters of a memoir, how to write from a place of honesty without getting disowned as a child.

Let me tell you what I found — it was not what I wanted. "The moment you write something your parents hate is the moment you've found your voice as a writer." Splendid! "As soon as you begin to write about your mother, you've lost." Terrific! "The day a writer is born into the family, the family is finished." How exciting! Writing, as I would come to learn in those arduous months of study, was a craft more destructive than murder.

Well, I must be a deranged killer. I must love peeling the skin off and examining what lies beneath — a modern day Michelangelo obsessed with his cadavers. Because give up writing, I could not.

During my last semester of college, I was selected to speak

171

on behalf of the Creative Writing department. Quite the contrary position to my vocal rebellion against organized education as a teenager, wouldn't you say? We were having an open house for parents to visit with their children, and it was my job to sell the parents. Sell them on what? It shouldn't surprise you to know that studying creative writing isn't exactly the most lucrative of degrees when it comes to financial stability. My own father, upon receiving my near-perfect college GPA in the mail said, "Just think, Cole. All these A's and you could have gone to medical school." These were not all writing classes either, if you were to attribute my success to an easy curriculum. I had an A in Environmental Science, an A in Honors History. Honors! When had I ever cared to take an honors class? Not in high school, I'll tell you that. And their argument against my playing the World of Warcraft so obsessively as an adolescent had always been that the game was keeping me from achieving my full potential — measured, of course, by a series of single letters placed beside each subject of study. I hate to shatter that misconception, but they had no idea upon my transferring to Columbia College Chicago and feeling utterly friendless, I started playing World of Warcraft again. I went back to sitting in front of my computer for upwards of three, four, five hours a day. Within a few months, I was right back to where I'd left off, competing with top-level players and wondering if I should pursue my dream of professional gaming once more. Yes, it was during my gaming comeback that I walked six blocks through the bitter Chicago cold to Math tutoring twice a week in the Student Center to ensure that I achieved another perfect semester.

When my parents saw the results, they said things like, "If only you could have been like this in high school. See, Cole? What's the difference between back then and now? Well, back then you were playing World of Warcraft and now you're not. Had you never played that game, you would have always been a straight A student."

I just kept my mouth shut. They were obviously blind to the other major fact that back then, I was clinically depressed from shitting daily bursts of blasphemous fecal fountains. More importantly, let us not forget that everything, all of my reality-based pursuits, school, the piano, were all done for them. I only became a straight A student when I wanted it for myself.

So who better than me, really, an esteemed and cultured senior, to speak to a room full of apprehensive parents and misunderstood children about the wonderful writing program at Columbia College Chicago? I believe I knew their predicament well. And what did I share with them, exactly? I told them my story. The one that just weeks prior had been published in the department's 2013 Story Week Reader. It was a very big deal. Only twenty-some stories were selected. My short was about the day I became one of the highest ranked World of Warcraft players in North America — and how, as a teenager, I came to the brutal realization that to my father and mother, my achievement would never be enough. It was a Story Week favorite. I celebrated alone. I couldn't tell my family. They would have been very disappointed in me.

But let me tell you, when I read that short story aloud again for all those parents and teenagers at the Open House, taking a stand for the right to write, I found the motivation to re-approach my entire book in the first person, facing my emotions head-on this time. The high school seniors seated before me, they knew of the game, World of Warcraft, had either played it themselves or at least heard of it. And the parents, oh they were furious, disappointment in their stares. Just minutes prior, they had seen me as the ultimate role model, someone they could only hope their own child would grow up to become, and here I was painting the all-too-misunderstood picture of what it was like to be one of the best in the world at something the majority of society believes to be an immeasurable waste of time. It was beautiful. I was shattering their glorified perceptions. I made sure to look certain parents dead, the angriest of the crowd, dead in the eyes as I drew parallels from the World of Warcraft to the real world, luminescent revelations lapping off my wicked tongue.

It's safe to say that quite a few parents in that audience realized through my story their own faults and judgments of their children. Whether they left that day with new intentions or not, I'll never know. But at least I made them take a look at themselves. And for every kid in that room, their chins in their hands looking up at me, I was doing it for them. If they couldn't get their parents to hear their hopes and dreams to do whatever they loved most in life, then maybe I could.

Afterwards, a kid with a few spots of acne and wrinkled clothes found me by the elevators. His parents were severely overweight. He was all smiles and just came right out with it. "What server did you play on?" I told him many. His parents were as eager. "Our son really enjoyed your story," the mother said. "He loves that game." I nodded, hoping I hadn't offended her in the process. "We'll keep an eye out for your book," said his short and stocky dad. And the kid, "I can't wait to read it!" Do you know what that was like? I saw myself in that kid. I look nothing how I used to — so much has changed — but that kid with the few spots of acne and the wrinkled clothes, that was me in high school. And it became all too clear in that moment: that's who I was writing for.

And I know what you're thinking (and I do realize that my saying this confirms your diagnosis of me; a narcissist, I'm sure): Why not just call the thing fiction and be done with it? A novel. Yes! Then all my narrative problems would be solved! Write the story that is mine, so real that one would question how a writer who is "not a soldier" could possibly describe the battlefield in such detail, but just before binding and placing it on the shelf, quickly hide behind the curtain that is every author's favorite veil. Fiction. Sigh. No! If I call this fiction, can you not see how I'll only be perpetuating the problem? None of this will be taken as real! Made up! Imaginary! It will be no more grounded in reality than the very video game and subsequent moral I am so desperately trying to discuss! And so the split will continue — real life and fantasy. The gap I am trying to bridge: Who the world believes I should be and who I truly am.

I know it might not seem all that important to most people, and I understand how ridiculous I must sound trying to make this point while blanketed in white privilege, of all things. But more than 12 million people played World of Warcraft. The lessons I learned in that game have been part of my life now for over 10 years. It was the only reason I didn't commit suicide as an awkward, insecure teenager. Some of the people I met online became my best friends — friends I still keep in contact with to this day. I know I'm not the only one who lived and died a member of the Horde. I know my parents weren't the only parents who wished their kid would spend less time in front of the computer. I know my wrinkled clothes and forehead full of acne were worn by hundreds of thousands of teenagers all over the world, and, if I'm being totally honest, while I am using personal examples and telling my individual story, this really isn't about my parents and this isn't about my rich town and this isn't even really about me or the World of Warcraft. This is about all of us. A generation of kids. Who are told every day of our lives to do what we love, and then chastised for our unique manifestation.

We're allowed to be anything we want — as long as it fits the mold.

Please understand, this is not a rage against their machine. This is not some irresponsible, immature rebellion with the hopes of me getting the last word in an argument. This is the honest song from a boy who learned at a very young age that success isn't found in a big house or an expensive car, or a "perfect family" with all the money in the world.

The true feeling of success is at the heart of what you love, and can be felt and found in as simple a thing as a video game.

Chapter 9
Like The Angel

Clapping

First Movement: Discover

In case you haven't picked up on it by now, the World of Warcraft is how I first discovered my voice. This one. Right here. The one you are hearing in your head as you read this. Can you hear it? LA LA LA. Do you hear that? The way I hear this voice in my head is the same way I hear my sister play the violin, sentences ringing off the walls of my cerebellum like melodies being rehearsed in our family room. The way I hear this voice is the same way I hear Mozart and Beethoven, Chopin and Bach. The way I hear this voice is, well, the same way I hear this...

[Guild][Hippykillers]: Hah, Sik that reminds me of the last blog you wrote. You should write more often!

[Guild][Sik]: I would if I didn't have to babysit this fucking guild. WHICH BY THE WAY, IF ANY OF YOU FUCKERS FORGOT YOUR FLASKS FOR THE RAID I'M GOING TO BE REALLY FUCKING PISSED.

[Guild][Hippykillers]: Charmayne and I read the last few blogs together and laughed our asses off.

[Guild][Sik]: Thank you, Hippy. And I'm sorry for calling you a smelly cunt earlier.

[Guild][Exitec]: You have a blog?

[Guild][Hippykillers]: It's hilarious. You would love it.

[Guild][Exitec]: Where can I find it?

[Guild][Sik]: Don't tell him, he'll ruin it somehow.

[Guild][Exitec]: How am I gonna ruin it?

[Guild][Sik]: Your parents will probably catch you reading it and then find a way to send me to jail.

[Guild][Cachexic]: I could totally see that happening.

[Guild][Revenance]: THIS JUST IN – SUBURBAN PARENTS SEND WoW GUILD LEADER TO JAIL, MORE AT 10!

[Guild][Exitec]: Guys, my parents aren't THAT bad.

[Guild][Sik]: Let's take a vote. Who here thinks Firefag's parents are psychotic?

[Guild][Charmayne]: I don't know his parents.

[Guild][Fatehand]: Def psychotic.

[Guild][Cachexic]: Cole, what the fuck are you talking about? You're ALWAYS bitching about your parents.

[Guild][Exitec]: Well yeah but I don't think they would ever freak out over something like a blog.

[Guild][Sik]: I beg to differ.

[Guild][Exitec]: I wanna read it

[Guild][Sik]: No

[Guild][Cachexic]: Cole, get on AIM. I'll send you a link.

[Guild][Sik]: GOD DAMMIT CACHE

[Guild][Exitec]: Cool, thanks.

[Guild][Sik]: Firefag I swear to god if I go to jail...

[Guild][Exitec]: Why would you go to jail? Do you write about bad stuff?

[Guild][Sik]: That's a loaded question, seeing as your parents' definition of bad includes everything except Christianity.

[Guild][Exitec]: I'm Catholic.

[Guild][Sik]: Same shit.

[Guild][Cachexic]: His blog is actually pretty funny. I read it sometimes when I'm taking a dump.

[Guild][Sik]: Thank you for that riveting testimonial, Cache.

[Guild][Cachexic]: Hey, it's the best time to read.

[Guild][Revenance]: Wail, it really is.

[Guild][Cachexic]: Until you get wrapped up in whatever you're reading and then you forget you're on the toilet and your legs go numb and you can't stand up.

[Guild][Sik]: I take it that's happened more times than one?

[Guild][Cachexic]: Daily, actually.

[Guild][Hippykillers]: Cole, I could see you really liking Sik's writing.

[Guild][Sik]: Of course he's going to like it.

[Guild][Cachexic]: You're so modest.

[Guild][Sik]: Not because I'm awesome. Even though I am. But because I write about a bunch of shit he's been deprived of his whole life.

[Guild][Exitec]: Like what?

[Guild][Sik]: You ever have a threesome with one girl

179

licking the inside of your butthole while the other one's blowing you so hard tears are streaming down her cheeks?

[Guild][Hippykillers]: That post was hilarious!

[Guild][Exitec]: I can't say that I have, no.

[Guild][Sik]: Of course you haven't.

[Guild][Cachexic]: I don't know that's typical human behavior, Sik.

[Guild][Revenance]: I've done it.

[Guild][Sik]: See? Rev's done it.

[Guild][Cachexic]: Hah, Rev you dirty fucking liar.

[Guild][Revenance]: Ok fine I haven't done it.

[Guild][Sik]: Oh. Well shit. I don't know, just don't jerk off to it or anything.

[Guild][Exitec]: Pinky promise on the no jerking.

[Guild][Sik]: Sometimes I wonder how I play this game sober

[Guild][Cachexic]: You don't play this game sober

[Guild][Fatehand]: At least you have me

[Guild][Sik]: Fatehand, you have bangs down to your nose and you wear black eyeliner. You're the reason why my alcohol consumption has tripled in the past two months. Go write Linkin Park lyrics on your wall or something.

[Guild][Charmayne]: LOL REKT

[Guild][Exitec]: I'm going to read a few posts. Be back in a bit.

[Guild][Revenance]: See ya, kowlie powlie.

[Guild][Hippykillers]: Have fun!

[Guild][Sik]: If Firefag ever makes something of himself, I'm taking full credit for introducing him to a world of artistry he'd never otherwise have been exposed to.

[Guild][Cachexic]: You can't claim credit for my Padawan.

[Guild][Revenance]: I'm still pretty pissed I never got a Padawan slave.

[Guild][Sik]: MY BLOG WILL INSPIRE HIM TO DO GREAT THINGS.

[Guild][Cachexic]: Like have dirty bathroom sex with hookers?

[Guild][Sik]: Precisely.

I went downstairs to grab my dad's laptop, and during that night's intestinal warfare session I sat on the cold porcelain toilet and explored Sik's blog.

It was unlike anything I'd ever read before in my life.

I had always found the reading we had to do for school to be quite boring: *Johnny looked like an oak tree in a willow wood as he stood in the dusk of what appeared to be his own desire. His desire, the same desire that had once perused his open mind and shallow heart from which he ran every night into seclusion. He was both his future self and the seed of his past, reaching for the sun as limbs do for warm greatness, gesturing to the heavens that all he could imagine and all he could fathom were breaths he still needed to take as he meandered down his path toward the infinite.* I would get one paragraph into a 300 page novel forced upon me by a less-than-enthusiastic English teacher and be completely clueless as to where we were; who was Johnny; why is he a tree; can someone please just explain to me where he's headed and why I should care.

But Sik's blog? Sik's blog was the first piece of writing that made me enjoy reading. It was loud. It was purposeful. It possessed a total disregard for punctuation and grammatical correctness. Every paragraph was a public declaration of power, every image crafted to teleport you to a separate reality — the bottom of a whiskey glass, an armchair placed in front of the television on Super Bowl Sunday, the grimy floor of a gas station bathroom and the echoing slurps of Asian twins. The sentences sang in my head. It sounded exactly like how Sik spoke in Ventrilo. This was his voice on paper. It was sarcastic, it was aggressive, and it moved without apology.

It was the coolest writing voice I'd ever heard.

And I wanted it.

Second Movement: Define

Yes! It's true! This vulgar, obscene, verbal diarrhea was the thunderbolt that struck my seed of rebellious artistry and set its growth ablaze! Imitation was my beginning! I was Mark Twain with the racial slang, Nabokov yelling "Fuck off!" Every time I took a shit, I brought in my dad's laptop with me and read Sik's blog. Whenever I had a free moment in the computer lab at school, I pulled up another post. Every spare moment I had outside of playing World of Warcraft was spent studying Sik's writing style. I couldn't get enough. I chewed on it. I digested it. And then I began to emulate it, spewing it everywhere.

My school papers, essays and homework assignments turned into opportunities to practice. Every short answer test question was a stage upon which I performed my language dance. Just like Sik, I stopped using commas all together. I wrote sentences so long that my teachers, aghast, pulled me aside to again remind me that there were rules to writing Cole and one must follow the rules if one wishes to become a talented writer but I told them no no error here Miss McKinsey see this is how I want the sentence to read because this sentence has personality and this sentence has a voice and this is my voice so if you'd kindly stop placing little red comma marks all over my paper I'd really appreciate it because to be perfectly honest art doesn't have rules and art doesn't have restrictions so the fact that you think there is some long list of guidelines that I have to follow in order to earn the mass approval of my writing just shows that you're not much of writer at all.

Teachers started calling home. "What do you mean our son refuses to follow the rules of the assignment?" Second semester junior year was no time to be messing around. We needed a turnaround and we needed one fast. My worried mother and disappointed father promptly hired me a tutor. The ACT was right around the corner and college applications were due shortly after.

In the front hallway of our abundant household stood a young Indian man with long scraggly hair. His T-shirt was two sizes too big and his jeans had a few tiny white paint stains on them, near the pockets. His gym shoes were extremely old and dirty, his smile brighter than the sun's reflection on snow.

[Abass]: "Hey Cole. Nice to meet you."

[Me]: "Yeah."

I wasn't very enthusiastic. I didn't need a tutor.

We took a seat at the dining room table. On the walls were paintings my mother had ordered from Rome. The nearby mantle was covered in rich candles and precious chocolates in little glass dishes. Abass let his eyes wander.

I let my backpack fall from my shoulder and slam on the long oak table.

[Me]: "Well, here's all my stuff."

"Why don't you tell me a bit about yourself," he said, pulling out a chair and taking a seat. He had a crinkled spiral notebook in one hand and a pen that had lost its cap in the other.

"Like what?"

"Anything! What's your favorite subject?"

"I don't have a favorite. I sort of hate them all."

"Ok, well which one do you hate the least?"

I thought about it.

"English, I guess. I really like writing."

"What do you like to write about?"

"Things I experience, mostly."

"There are some really great writing colleges out there," he said.

"Writing colleges? What do you mean?"

"Colleges where you can study writing," he said.

"You can study writing in college?"

He laughed.

"Of course!"

"Just writing?"

"Well, you'll have to take a few general classes, like everyone else, but yes. Your major can be writing."

"But is it boring writing? Like Shakespeare writing?"

"Probably some essays here and there, but there are creative writing programs too."

I fell back into my chair, amazed.

"And all my classes can be writing classes?" I said, reiterating this elusive, creative future no one had ever presented as a viable option.

"After you get your general classes out of the way, sure."

In my mind, writing was the easiest thing in the world — especially since I could type 120+ words per minute. By studying writing in college, I would be able to breeze through all my homework assignments and then have hours upon hours free, in my dorm room, to play World of Warcraft.

I didn't really want to become a writer.

What I wanted was to become a professional gamer.

After I hit level 70 in the World of Warcraft expansion, I started playing the new 2v2, 3v3, and 5v5 arenas. The arena system was very different than the Honor system. It was a ladder, each team starting at a rating of 1500. In each bracket — 2v2, 3v3, 5v5 — you were then paired against teams with similar ratings, the winning team gaining points, the losing team losing points. The higher you climbed in rating — 1600, 1700, 1800, etc. — you were then paired against better and better players.

The caveat to the arena system was that there weren't always teams queuing at your rating. So if you were a 1900 3v3 team and there were no other ~1900 teams queuing up, then the system would either pair you with a team rated much higher, ~2100, or much lower, ~1700. If a 1900 team beat another 1900 team, the winning team got 15 points added onto their rating, and the losing team would lose 15 points from their rating. But if a 1900 team beat a 2100 team, one that was clearly ranked much higher, then the 1900 team could earn upwards of 30 points, and the 2100 team would lose that same amount. Conversely, if the 2100 team beat a 1900 team, they may only gain 5 points, and the 1900 team may only lose 5 points, because the system understood that it was not a very even match up. As a result, the higher you climbed, the more stressful arenas became. You had far more to lose than you had to gain.

Of course, a high arena rating meant access to rare and powerful rewards. Each week, on Tuesday when the servers went down for maintenance, players received a certain number of arena points based on their highest arena rating in any bracket. Higher ratings yielded more points; lower ratings, less points. Arena points could then be spent on arena gear and weapons, which were specifically made for PvP combat — and also looked incredibly cool on your character. At the end of each arena season, which was

3-4 months long, the top .5% of players in each Battlegroup (made up of 9+ severs) were given the highly coveted title of Gladiator, along with the rare flying mount for that season.

This was the real incentive to play arenas. Bragging rights. In the World of Warcraft, to become a Gladiator was to become a God.

Cachexic had made it abundantly clear that his only goal was to become the highest ranked Mage in 3v3 arenas. He had absolutely no interest in going off to college. A year older than me, he warned of the slow agonizing torture that came with ACT testing and college applications. Instead, he applied to community college and decided he was going to live at home for a year.

"Why the fuck would I go sit in more classes I hate when I can make a living doing something I love," he said. And I agreed.

In March, 2007, a major sponsor named CheckSix Gaming picked up its first World of Warcraft team. CheckSix also sponsored Counterstrike, Call of Duty, and BF1942 teams, and adding 5v5 arena team ZERG IT DOWN to its roster only confirmed the community's speculations: World of Warcraft would soon become a mainstream e-sport.

Cachexic and I saw this as our opportunity. We had spent the past three years of our lives mastering the game, and were on the cusp of its explosion. We were pioneers, perfectly positioned to take advantage of this budding industry, and both made a conscious decision to pursue professional gaming as a career.

At the same time, <Loot Crusade> had decided to take a break after rushing through all the new raid content in the expansion. Revenance, too, was applying to college and had less and less time to play the game. He decided to sell his account on eBay for $900 and use that money toward buying a car. He said goodbye to the World of Warcraft once and for all.

With no one to hold us back, Cachexic and I transferred to arguably the most competitive server in North America: Blackrock.

At the time, Blackrock housed some of the best players in the country, and if we wanted to turn pro, then we needed to compete against the best of the best.

Blackrock is where I ultimately began my rampant rise to fame on the Internet.

My first week on the server, while playing 3v3 arenas, I faced off against a well-known Undead Mage named Sunburn. A little backstory on Sunburn: His name was originally Pigvomit, and was famous in the Mage community for making PvP videos, similar to Cachexic. As a result, both he and Cachexic were often mentioned in people's "Best Mage Of All Time?" forum threads. Cachexic, however, thought Sunburn was a disgrace to the art of the game and the Mage class (and I'm sure Sunburn said the same about him). They were rivals in every sense, and the moment we stepped foot on Blackrock, that rivalry was palatable.

The fact that I ended up getting matched to face Sunburn was a perfect example of the arena ladder's still very buggy system. I had average gear, and so did my teammates. We were ranked ~1700. Sunburn, on the other hand, was one of the highest rated Mages on Blackrock in all three brackets: 2v2, 3v3, and 5v5. He had the best gear in the game, and a top-tier 3v3 team that looked like it was on track to hit Gladiator the first season. He was ranked ~2100.

The game should have been over in less than 30 seconds, and instead lasted almost 20 minutes. Sunburn and his teammate, a Warlock named Breathless, could not land a kill. They chased me all over the map, trying to lock me in a Frost Nova for a Shatter combo kill. But I had spent so many hours dueling Cachexic that I knew how to outmaneuver any Mage. I would fake Sunburn's casts. I would force his Silences. I would make it seem like I was going to run right into his trap, and then Blink through him a millisecond before his Frost Nova/Silence, my character whipping around the corner and out of danger.

Even though we ultimately lost, immediately after the game I received a private message from Breathless.

[Breathless] whispers: Hey, you got a sec?

[Exitec] whispers: Sure, what's up?

[Breathless] whispers: First of all, good game. That was a fun one.

[Exitec] whispers: Thanks. You too.

[Breathless] whispers: How come you aren't higher rated?

[Exitec] whispers: Eh, I'm still working on getting better gear. I only hit level 70 a couple weeks ago.

[Breathless] whispers: I see.

[Breathless] whispers: Well look, I was really impressed with the way you played that last game. I've never seen a Mage avoid damage like that before. And I feel like if we helped you get your arena gear set you would be unstoppable.

I couldn't believe what I was hearing.

[Exitec] whispers: But isn't Sunburn your Mage?

[Breathless] whispers: Lol, that dude is the most overrated player I've ever seen. We're only playing with him because he has top quality gear. But we know we'll never hit Gladiator with him.

[Exitec] whispers: It would take a few weeks for me to get geared up though, maybe longer.

[Breathless] whispers: We're willing to make the investment.

[Exitec] whispers: Well shit. Yeah man, I'd love to play with you guys. Do you want me to leave my team so you can invite me to yours?

[Breathless] whispers: Yup. I just kicked Sunburn. Let me know when you're ready for an invite.

You have joined 3v3 team: Conquered Ur Mom!

188

Word spread like wildfire that Sunburn had been kicked from his own team, and that I was the Mage to replace him. A Mage without a single piece of arena gear. Even Cachexic was dumbfounded that I'd leapt so high up the ladder, so fast. But like a proud father, he congratulated me on my achievement.

"You deserve it," he said.

"Thanks man, that means a lot," I said, sitting in my computer chair, eating a chocolate chip muffin (wheat).

"I remember when you were just lil' baby Firephunk," said Cachexic, making his voice high-pitched, as if talking to a child.

"Hey, you're the reason I made it this far," I said. I meant it too.

"I'll take some of the credit," he said. "But you were the one who listened. Very few people actually fucking listen. I'm proud of you."

In that moment, I knew. The student had surpassed the teacher.

Less than two weeks later, Cachexic quit the World of Warcraft. He couldn't find a good enough team to play with, and said he was bored of the game. The truth is, Cachexic couldn't adjust to the new expansion. The Mage class was very different now than it had been in years prior, and he struggled to adapt.

In an attempt to re-discover his gaming talents, he tried to trade his account for a different class — a Rogue. He insisted that Mages weren't what they used to be. This, to me, was a clear sign of my mentor's downfall. There had always been issues with the game, but this was the first time I had ever heard him speak with an acceptance of defeat. Instead of refining his playstyle and looking for a solution, he was trying to take the easy road.

For Cachexic, this rash decision was the nail on the coffin. The trade ended up being a scam, and his original account was stolen. His Mage was gone to the digital ether, unrecoverable. In an instant, he lost thousands of hours of work and one hell of a valuable character.

It should come as no surprise that Cachexic got severely depressed and vanished. He stopped answering his phone or his AIM messages. For a while, I legitimately wondered if he had killed himself — his character meaning more to him than anything else in his life. When he did finally return a few weeks later, he was different. Very different. He spoke with slowed speech, and constantly excused himself to smoke another bowl. He had picked up smoking weed as a habit, and the majority of our conversations now consisted of his reasons why I should quit the World of Warcraft and start smoking weed too. He hoped that I would join him in his misery.

I knew if I wanted to become a professional gamer, I would have to do it on my own.

Third Movement: Design

By the time my junior year came to a close, I was ranked in the top 100 3v3 teams in the country, with an arena rating of ~2300. My Mage was decked from head to toe in the best gear in the game. I had more gold in my pockets than I'd ever had in my entire life, other players paying me in-game currency to help increase their own ratings in other arena brackets like 2v2 or 5v5. Some days, I would log into the game after school and just stare at my Undead Mage in the character selection screen. He was everything I had ever wanted to be: A perfect representation not of the scraggly haired boy sitting in his computer chair, but the soul inside.

On Blackrock, with my charcoal black robes and glowing red staff, I was a celebrity.

Everybody knew my name.

When school finally let out for summer, I found myself with little else to do in the World of Warcraft except play arenas. Being a hardcore gamer though, I still wanted to spend time in front of my computer. I started reading a lot of guild forums, gaming blogs, and discovered that some of the top players had personal blogs where they shared tips about the game, stories, match recaps, etc. There was one blog that interested me the most, and was by a Human Rogue named Ming.

Ming was a ~2300 player as well, and wrote daily blogs about his high rated arena matches. I saw his blog as a resource where I could keep up with the strategies of other top players, and would often read it in the morning while I ate my eggs on toast for breakfast (wheat).

That summer, Ming made a public announcement on his personal website that he would be making the move to a new blogging site for gamers called GameRiot, posting content there exclusively. As a loyal reader, I followed.

What made GameRiot cool was that it had social media elements that created the feeling of community. Keep in mind this was 2007, when MySpace was headed out the door, Facebook was still very new, and the idea of "blogging" was not yet mainstream or popular.

GameRiot was a platform built for gamers, specifically World of Warcraft players. You could browse the site as a reader, or you could create your own blog and become a contributor. New blogs were automatically posted to the front page news feed, and on the right-hand side of the screen was a ladder of the Top 10 Most Popular Bloggers on the site, based on how many views their blogs received. It was a writing platform, but gamified in a way that encouraged competition.

Intrigued, I decided to give it a try. It was a Saturday afternoon, the rest of my family in the backyard swimming in our pool. I could hear them through my open window, laughing, splashing water, music playing from the outdoor speakers. The breeze came into my room and invited me outside. Instead, I stayed in my room. I logged into the World of Warcraft and ran my character to the Hall of Legends in Orgrimmar, where I sat with the draping backdrop of the Horde flag behind me. I took a screenshot on my computer, and used this screenshot as my profile picture on

GameRiot.

I named my blog *Exitec Style*.

My intention was to create something similar to Ming's blog. I wanted to be an educational resource for gamers interested in improving their gameplay. I had a vast working knowledge of the World of Warcraft and thought that high-end information about arenas would be valuable to share — my credibility as a writer reinforced by the fact that I was one of the highest rated Mages currently playing the game. In some sense, I saw having a blog on GameRiot as one more step toward making World of Warcraft my career. If I could position myself as a thought leader in the community, that would only open the door to more sponsorship and tournament opportunities.

Below is my very first blog post, my first piece of writing shared publically on the Internet, saved, copy and pasted from 2007, grammatical errors and all:

STYLE

By: Exitec

After many months of waiting for this new "WoW e-sport" website to finally get off the ground, I can say im very happy so far with how gameriot.com has been running. It gives a lot of people their chance at being able to talk about what they want to talk about, and hopefully this website will bring a new style to the game we all love to play.

As a little introduction, this blog will be heavily focused on not only arena PvP from a mages perspective, but also just PvP in general. I have been playing the mage class since closed BETA of WoW, and have leveled 4 up to 60, one up to 70. Pre-BC the highest I grinded was up to rank 11, and post BC i've taken part in many 2k+ rated arena teams; 3s being my favorite and most competative bracket.

As for the past few years of playing WoW, you name the server, and i've probably leveled a mage there. I've

192

played with big name guilds such as A-Team (stormreaver), Nocturnal (stormscale), Blacklisted (wildhammer), Loot Crusade (Black Dragonflight), Unfadable (laughing skull), Mediocrity (blackrock), and Militia (frostmane). As for the players i've competed against, many come from such guilds as Vicious Cycle (frostmane), Forgotten Hero's (black dragonflight), In Excelsis (laughing skull), Impervious (stormreaver), Deux Vox (laughing skull), and Eminence (blackrock). The reason I re-rolled so many times was for exactly this reason; before you could server transfer, I re-rolled to face new competition. To this day I still hop on the test realms to fight those I used to play with/against, and it makes for some great competition.

After playing with what I consider to be some of the top names in WoW, i've learned that in order to set yourself apart from every other run of the mill player (or mage in this case), you need to develop your own style. A lot of people prefer to make their style to be as flashy as possible, especially video makers. Although it looks nice when your tearing bads apart, it can often cost you the fight against another well skilled opponent. You need to remember that somewhere in your style your playing to win, and not just show off; something that took me a long time to really understand.

Hopefully this blog will give some insight to players looking to set themselves apart from the rest of the crowd. Arenas are just as competative as any sport i've ever played IRL, and god knows losing in WoW can feel just as bad as losing a championship hockey game as well.

-Exitec-

70 Undead Mage

<Blackrock>

Stop by and say hello!

Fourth Movement: Develop

Since I was one of the first active writers on GameRiot, my

blog gained immediate traction. One of the moderators commented saying that he really enjoyed my writing style and looked forward to reading more of my material. Of course, as a seventeen year old I had no concept of this being a strategic move on his part to keep me interested in creating content for the site. I just thought he was being honest and genuinely thought my writing was awesome. This was more than enough encouragement to keep me coming back day after day.

Blogging on GameRiot quickly became an obsession of mine. It was the gamification element that motivated me, this idea that my writing could be "better" than someone else's and ranked on the front page. Every night, I would look at who the top bloggers were, Ming always sitting at number 1, and then I would attempt to write something worthy of getting my name on that list.

Since I was simultaneously competing in very high rated arenas, I often used that day's games as inspiration. I would write about the teams we faced, the strategies that had led us to victory or the missteps and tough lessons we had learned through numerous losses. I tried, as best I could, to maintain a strict focus on the game, teaching other players how to improve and one day make it to the top.

However, I noticed that Ming began taking a very different approach to his blog. He no longer wrote as much about top-tier gameplay. Instead, he became a behind-the-scenes journalist for the drama that unfolded between top players. He would write about rivalries between teams, or expose players' personal lives — and even started writing about his own personal life, his love life, and his soon-to-be-wife. His blog ended up having very little to do with the World of Warcraft, and was much more of a public journal for the man behind the character.

And week after week, he was the most read blogger on the site.

One day, I decided to go out on a limb and take a different approach to my blog. Clearly what I was doing wasn't working — I had yet to have my name make it to the Top 10 list. Instead of writing about that day's 3v3 matches and the teams we faced, I wrote about the labels placed upon gamers by mainstream society. How gamers are seen as antisocial and socially inept, and how in reality we are simply misunderstood. I spoke of the similarities between gaming and playing a sport like hockey. I made mention of how ridiculous it is that football players are praised for playing a game, but gamers are condemned. And I ended my essay with a Call To Arms for all gamers to stand up for what they love, and to never let anyone tell them that gaming is in any way a lesser pursuit.

The comments section exploded. Some shared praise, others called me a fucking idiot, and sub-discussions between readers went on for pages and pages. Everyone seemed to have an opinion on the topic and my blog post had opened the door for readers to share their own thoughts. It was one of GameRiot's most popular blog posts for weeks. And for the first time, my name was on the Top 10 Most Read list, right under Ming's, at number 2.

From that moment on, I barely wrote about the intricacies of the game. Instead, I wrote about the idea of gaming, society's expectations, and what it was like to be a top-tier gamer in a world that saw video games as a complete and utter waste of time. My voice was a blend between Ming's thought leadership and Sik's raw, unfiltered prose. I saw myself as a spokesperson for the entire World of Warcraft community, and gave voice to every pissed off teenager and reclusive gamer.

Every single night for that entire summer, before my senior year of high school, I would finish playing competitive arenas around two or three in the morning and then I would write the next morning's blog. Sitting up in my bed, my dad's laptop on my lap, I would take my stand on the Internet. I would inspire. I would rage. I would write and write and write, and then diligently review each blog post's performance the next day, letting the applause dictate what I wrote about next.

Over time, the answer became obvious: Readers didn't care about how much more damage they could do per second if they stacked Haste instead of Crit. They didn't care about healing rotation interrupt sequences or what the perfect counterstrategy was against Warlock, Rogue, Shaman. Readers wanted controversy. They wanted drama. They wanted vulgar, obscene, "fuck you society." They wanted to know that somewhere out there in the real world was someone, just like them, with the confidence to say the things they were all feeling but were too afraid to say themselves.

They wanted to feel heard.

I knew my readers well. Oh, I knew them so, so well.

So I gave them exactly what they wanted.

Fifth Movement: Deploy

Girls - So Fun To Post About

By: Exitec

Ok guys, let me tell you about my night.

After the most painful 2 hour phone conversation of my entire life, I could do nothing but walk to my computer and express my feelings over the interweb. This phone conversation did nothing but tear my brain apart in ways I never thought imaginable, and the only thing I wanted to do was hang up, but was left with no opportunity to do so. Congratulations Kayla, you just beat me at Phone PvP.

For those of you who love drama, I'll give you some background on Kayla. Kayla is the girl at school who is so gorgeous you don't even bother talking to her, is so rich that she drives a BMW Convertible to school, and is so fucking stupid she got a 16 on her ACT. But none of that matters, her ass is phenomenal, and she parties hard, so obviously she was worth a little effort and a few phone calls right? Wrong.

For those of you who got a kick out of my last article, I briefly touched on the "awkward party situation" but let me elaborate for all of you who are obviously sitting there a bit confused. This past weekend I attended the first real party of my senior year. The party to kick it all off, and the place where parent's weren't allowed and clothes were optional. After 1000 parties you would think I would have figured out how girls play their games, but it seems no matter how many times you try to sit there and figure them out, they always line of sight you (literally) and you end up sitting there with your dick in your hand, and no place to go. So after an hour or two, and a few beers and bowls in me, I decided to talk a walk around the house and see what everyone was up to...

5 minutes later my good friend Erica comes up and tells me Kayla has a thing for me, and she's drunk, and I should take advantage of her. Now, I'm not usually one to do such a thing to such an innocent girl, let alone waste my time with something that COULDN'T be true, but I decided to just engage in some nice, respectable conversation with her to see if I could get any information. I read her faster than Asia reads Ming's fucking blog. It was over, and I was bout to dominate this bitch 1v1.

(For all you sitting there jerking off at your computers at this point, I'll leave the details out so you are forced to close this page and go open up your favorite porno site to climax.)

Today, Thursday, 5 days after our little rendez-vous at El Party, I was forced to have my first real phone conversation with this girl. Before now, it had been nothing but mindless texts with "IDK MY BFF JILL" and things of the sort. However today, she felt it necessary to call me around 7pm (WHILE I WAS IN AN ARENA) and talk about her day. Now, let's just say the phone convo didn't start off well with me answering and yelling "I'LL CALL YOU BACK IN ONE SEC" and then hanging up, all while I finished casting my frostbolt. After the arena I of course called this inconsiderate b1tch back, and told my team I would be back in 10, assuming I'd listen to a few stories, and be on my way. Wrong.

To summarize the phone convo, it was nothing but her telling her stupid ass girl jokes that make no sense, and me having to use every ounce of energy to force out a laugh every 30 seconds. While I wasn't laughing (or at least trying to), I was forced to say things like "You're crazy! Hehe!" and "Wow no way!" which

197

made me feel about as gay as Ryan Seacrest. Let me tell you, hanging off a girl's ovaries for 2 hours, is no fun.

So why did I endure all this pain? No, it wasn't the hookup, and no she's not smart in any way, shape, or form. But I do know that later tonight when her away message on aim goes up, and she leaves my name and a few XOXOXOXOXOXO's in there, I'll get to listen to every guy go, "SOAH BRO I NOTICED KAYLA GAVE YOU A FEW HUGS N KISSES IN HER AWAY MESSAGE? SUP WIT DAT BRAH" in which case I will calmly respond, "yeah we spent a few hours together last night, if you know what I mean."

Congrats Kayla, you just wrecked my face in Phone PvP, but when it comes to AIM PvP, you better be ready, or your vagina is gonna get real sandy, real fast.

...

...

...I know what you're thinking.

Who on God's green earth would ever enjoy reading that?

I'll tell you exactly who: Seventeen-year-old kids playing World of Warcraft.

About 10,000 of them. Every single day.

I became one of GameRiot's most popular bloggers for over a year straight.

I was a writer after all.

Chapter 10
Take Cover (Bonus Track)

Q: I never knew that about you. And this was all before Rose, right?

A: Yeah, way before Rose. Everything I was writing on the Internet was made up, for the most part. I wasn't chatting on AIM with any girls — I'd never even had a girlfriend. I was just a kid sitting on the toilet with his dad's laptop imagining what it would be like, writing fiction.

Q: If you were seeing so much success with it, how come you didn't keep it up? Because I remember Freshman year of college you were still playing World of Warcraft a bit, but I never saw you writing.

A: That's a great question — and trust me, I still wonder today how far I could have taken it. Back in 2007, nobody thought building a career for yourself on the Internet was possible, especially in gaming. But if you look at the famous gaming YouTubers and streamers today, they are doing exactly what I was doing ten years ago, just on video. Some of them take the educational route, teaching other gamers how to play at the highest level. Some take the entertainment route and create videos they know will make people laugh or start drama. Either way, at the core they are all doing the same thing: they are branding themselves — and that's what I was doing, in my own weird way, as a teenager.

So, you know. Every once in a while I think about that. In 2007, I saw where everything was going. I saw how powerful having a personal brand could be, it's just the Internet wasn't quite mature enough yet. That sort of monetization in the gaming space didn't really start to happen until 2010, 2011.

Why I stopped playing World of Warcraft and why I ultimately stopped writing had nothing to do with my doubting if I could make gaming a viable career. I was very much in a position to succeed in that industry, and knew I was on the path to Success. The reason why I stopped had a lot more to do with what was going on within me at the time, emotionally. When I graduated high school and left home for the University of Missouri, I was not in a healthy place — at all.

Q: And why was that? What happened?

A: It was a combination of a lot of things.

First of all, let me tell you exactly how I achieved the title of Gladiator in the game, and then I'll explain what that sort of achievement did to me.

The first semester of my senior year of high school was insane. This was really the final challenge for me, testing to see how badly I wanted to obtain Success in the World of Warcraft. My parents were so worried that I wasn't going to get into a good college, they legitimately thought my only option would be to attend the local community college, which my high school peers had so eloquently nicknamed the "College of Dreams," since that's where dreams went to die. What nobody seemed willing to acknowledge, however, was that a C average at my rich, white high school was like a B+ average at most other high schools in the country. I wasn't all that worried. I knew I'd get in somewhere.

Still, my parents did everything possible to ensure that I spent as little time in front of my computer as possible. I had a tutor on Saturdays for the ACT, another tutor twice a week for Math and Science. I had started playing hockey again for the school hockey team so I could put on my resumé that I was an athlete — which only lasted half the season since I ended up reinjuring my spine. I had college applications to fill out. I had an ACT practice class on Wednesday nights. And after dinner, five days a week, my dad

200

would come home from work, grab his late plate from the counter, and call me over to the kitchen table to drill Algebra equations or Chemistry flashcards. I give my dad a lot of credit, honestly. After a ten-hour day in the operating room he would still sit down with me to make sure I was prepared for my next test. Just goes to show how much he cared about my future.

At the same time, my parents had also started to remind me that college was not free and I needed to get a job and save up some money. Obviously, being the entrepreneurial young spirit that I was, my first thought was to find a way to make money off my gaming blog. I did some searching around online and stumbled across this website that offered to pay writers to contribute World of Warcraft walkthrough guides for new players. I sent in an application and less than five minutes later received an e-mail back from the owner of the website. Turns out, he was a huge fan of my blog and instantly offered me a paid writing gig. $50 an article, three articles a week — and I could easily write an article in less than thirty minutes.

Well, the next week, when I received my first paycheck via my dad's PayPal account, my dad flipped out — and not in a good way. He thought I was doing something illegal on the Internet, stealing money. Again, looking back, I understand. It was a generational gap. But at the time, I was so upset. I even showed him the articles I had written as proof, trying to explain that the author's alias, Exitec, was me, Cole! But this only worried him and my mother more. They were terrified that I believed making money on the Internet was an intelligent long-term play.

They made me get a "real job" instead. I started working 20 hours a week scooping ice cream at the local Coldstone Creamery making $7.25 an hour. To put things in perspective, I was making 5x that writing articles about World of Warcraft online — and writing was something I genuinely enjoyed doing.

My sister, Brooke, on the other hand, was using her passion and primary skill set, the violin, to make money playing gigs — which was, for some reason, completely acceptable to both my parents. She would play for dinner parties, for little fundraisers,

201

getting paid $100 for a few hours of Mozart, to which my mother gave her nothing but approval. "See? Do you see how Brooke is using something she loves to make a living? That's the life of an artist!" And I would sulk my way over to the island counter, grab the keys to my BMW, and drive to Coldstone Creamery to scoop ice cream for four hours because writing about video games wasn't considered "artistic" enough.

Q: That must have been really hard for you. How did that make you feel?

A: Honestly? I hated my parents. That's a strong word, but if I'm being honest, as a teenager I really did hate them. Here I was, one of the best gamers in the world — not the town, not the state, not the Midwest, not the country, the fucking *world* — with my sights set on creating my own career, doing what I loved, and they didn't give it an ounce of approval. Not even a "good job, Cole." Nothing. They didn't try to understand it. They didn't respect it. They just chalked the whole thing up to rebellion and insisted that I pursue something different. And I just kept thinking, hoping, "Maybe if I climb higher, maybe if I'm not in the top .5% but the top .1% or the top .01%, then they'll see me. Then they'll acknowledge me." I just kept raising the bar for myself, desperately chasing any sort of validation that I was, in this game of life and in the eyes of my parents, a player of value.

So, that's what I was dealing with my senior year of high school. All of those expectations to succeed, while working a shitty part-time job when I had a more enjoyable and profitable option readily available, while studying for the ACT, while researching colleges and going on college visits with my mom, while studying subjects I despised with my tutor, while studying more subjects I despised with my dad, and somehow, at least three nights out of every week there was still time for my parents to call me into the living room and speak to me, with great duress, their ever-escalating fears that I was not headed in the direction of Success — for upwards of two to three hours; I am not joking. We would sit there in the living room, and they would go on, and on, and on, reminding me that I was not putting in the time or the effort required to Succeed. I remember sitting there wondering, night after night, if they ever thought about how much time they were taking away from my time studying, reminding me that I should spend more time studying. I won't lie, I saw the whole thing through a lens of dark humor.

Oh, and let's not forget that I had yet to be diagnosed with Celiac Disease. So, in addition to all the above, I was constantly shitting my brains out, and I was coping by not eating between the hours of breakfast and dinner.

And still! Every single day, every single night, after 8 hours of school, and then hockey practice, and then studying with my tutor, or working at Coldstone Creamery, and then drilling flashcards before bed with my dad, and then talking to both my parents in the living room, or their master bedroom, once again this feeling of "not being good enough" branded deeper and deeper my psyche, I returned to my bed, pretended to sleep for fifteen or twenty minutes, and then tip-toed over to my computer where I would play 3v3 arenas against the best players in North America until two in the morning, log off, grab my dad's laptop, and let my fingers roar through another blog post before catching five hours of sleep and doing the whole thing over again.

Q: That's really intense, and definitely not sustainable. How did you keep yourself motivated to keep going?

A: I wanted to prove my parents wrong. That's really it. I was driven by pure anger. I wanted to show them that what I was doing was real, it had potential, it was what I loved and I could make it work — I knew I could. I didn't even want to go to college. I had zero interest in sitting in another class, with another teacher, teaching me another thing to memorize that I would never use in my day-to-day life. It was pointless to me, relative to what I wanted to spend my life doing. The only reason I actually ended up going to college was because my dad was paying for the whole thing, and I knew I needed to get out of the house. It was such an unhealthy environment for me that I was willing to do whatever it took to leave.

Q: Ok, so senior year of high school, all these things are happening at once. When did you actually achieve the title of Gladiator and what was that like?

A: Well, I was supposed to have gotten Gladiator the first arena season, the summer before my senior year. But once our team hit a certain rating, basically Breathless and Eraticstate stopped playing. They wanted to just wait the rest of the season out, since we were guaranteed to get the title.

But since Breathless and Eraticstate were both from New Zealand and lived in a different time zone, I would often leave our 3v3 team to go play with other people for fun, since we weren't always online at the same time. Lots of people team-hopped to practice, it wasn't really a big deal. But they didn't tell me when they were going to stop playing 3v3 and just sit on the rating. So one day, when I asked them to invite me back to the team, they told me they weren't going to play any more games and were going to wait out the rest of the season. Basically, I was shit out of luck — because once you left the team, your personal rating got wiped.

With no real team and everybody waiting the first season out, I decided to transfer servers at the end of the summer. I went to a tiny server called The Underbog, because Ez, Maull, and Clitauren had all come back to the game and decided to play there for fun. I went to join them, since they were really the only friends I had left in the game.

There, I ended up meeting a Rogue by the name of Escape, who was extremely high rated in the 2v2 bracket, with a Priest named Telani. Apparently, The Underbog had a shortage of good Mages, and as soon as I arrived they picked me up to play 3v3.

It was a perfect fit. Escape and Telani became my teammates my senior year of high school, and they were also a huge reason why I was able to stay so motivated. All three of us had somehow gotten screwed out of our Gladiator title Season 1, and were hell-bent on achieving Gladiator in Season 2. We exclusively played with each other — none of us team-hopped. It was us three and no one else.

204

By the time November rolled around, we were competing for the Number 1 spot in the Battlegroup. It was a Sunday night, and we were facing the Alliance 3v3 team currently ranked Number 1. Whoever won this game would be granted that top spot.

Thirty minutes in and the match was still going. There I sat, in front of my computer, headphones clasped around my head, my neck jutted forward and my eyes darting all across my screen, my fingers playing a minuet of Frostbolts and Polymorphs, Counterspells and Cone of Colds, when all of a sudden my door burst open. My two younger brothers, wielding Nerf guns, unloaded rounds of foam bullets at my head and screen, while at the same time singing, "It's time to take the recyclables out to the street! You're WoW'ing, but you're certainly not OWN-ing!"

I swear to you, I almost burst a blood vessel. Here I had the best Alliance Night Elf Rogue in our Battlegroup up my ass, Kicking every cast, while I was trying to land a Sheep on their Druid and Counterspell their Warlock's Fear so that our Priest wouldn't get Feared, Escape and Telani screaming expletives and calling swap targets in my headset, and at the same time I've got Nerf bullets hitting me in the side of the head while my little brothers are singing off-key about chores and recyclables and how I'm "*Certainly not own'ing,*" aka, not Succeeding in the World of Warcraft.

And who do you think wrote those clever lyrics? This was arguably the most important 3v3 match of my entire gaming career, and not only was I fending off an attack from my younger brothers, but I was also being mocked through the lyrics of their little song of the worthlessness of my endeavor from the very person I hoped deep down would one day give me his approval — my father.

Somehow, Escape and I caught their healer in a CC chain and landed a kill on their Rogue. I didn't celebrate. I immediately yanked my headphones off and leapt out of my computer chair, both my brothers suddenly realizing that their lives were in severe danger. Thomas, the more athletic brother, made a run for it, leaving Donald in his wake, from which a very beautiful memory has been forever engraved in my brain: Thomas at the top of the stairs,

205

looking down, Donald on the third step, looking up, reaching one arm up toward him, calling, begging for his brother to save him, while my hand grabs his shirt and yanks him back down to the ground again and Thomas runs to alert our parents.

I gave Donald the most painful wedgie of his entire life, his underwear being pulled so far up his back that we both heard it rip. He began to cry, and I could hear the footsteps of our guardians making their way to the scene to inform me that I had lost my mind, that I was the one in the wrong here, that if I was getting this upset about being disrupted while playing a "stupid computer game" then something was seriously wrong with me.

Q: Hahahaha. So then what happened? Did you end up hitting Number 1?

A: Based on that match, yes. In our Battlegroup, we were the Number 1 3v3 team, no question. But the next morning, I checked the rankings online, and the team we had beaten was suddenly a hundred and fifty points higher than us. It didn't make any sense. They were so far ahead of everyone else on the ladder that we knew they had cheated to get there.

This was really the turning point for us as a team, and where everything started to fall apart.

First of all, a few days later Telani's account got banned. He had decided to level up a second character for fun, and didn't want to spend a ton of time grinding honor gear in Battlegrounds, so he started using a mouse-clicker bot. A bot basically allowed you to set the coordinates of your mouse to click around the screen and automate the game. You could set it to talk to a Battlemaster, enter a Battleground, and then click around to make sure you didn't go AFK—that way you could just rack up Honor points. Technically, it was cheating, but a lot of players did it anyway because they could set the bot in the morning, go to work or school, and come home to a character with enough Honor points to buy a full set of Honor gear.

Blizzard Entertainment had caught wind of this happening,

206

and started using software to track people's clicking habits, banning players they thought were botting — and Telani was one of those players. His account got banned a week before Season two ended. And of course, since he was the current leader of our 3v3 team, our top-rated team also vanished.

Escape and I were furious. Somehow, we had to find a third player and grind up a new 3v3 team from ground zero again in less than a week.

We ended up recruiting a Druid that I had actually played with back on Wildhammer, two years prior. His name was Frappuccino. Again, out of sheer luck it was a perfect fit, and the first day we went almost undefeated. We climbed from the starting rating of 1500 to 2300 no problem. We were guaranteed to get Gladiator.

But seeing how close we were to that Number 1 spot, we all agreed that we wanted to go for it. The only problem was, the top 10 teams had all win-traded up to an absurd rating like 2450, 2500, and then decided to stop playing and wait out the end of the season. We couldn't surpass them. If we wanted to hit Number 1, then we were going to have to cheat too.

How win-trading worked was you would find another high-ranked team and pay them gold to purposefully lose to you, which made your rating go up. When I told Ez, Maull, and Clitauren the situation they were more than willing to help out, for free. What we did was, we helped them level up a 3v3 team to a high enough rating, and then one night at four thirty in the morning when nobody else was online, we all sat in Ventrilo together and queued our two teams up at the exact same time. Ez, Maull, and Clitauren just sat on the other end of the arena and let us win to collect our points, while we all laughed maniacally in Ventrilo together, sleep-deprived and drooling at the thought of being granted the most coveted title in the game. Teams that hit Number 1 in their Battlegroup were given the title of Merciless Gladiator.

When the sun came up and we had finished our deed, I logged offline and pulled up the Arena Rankings web page for our

Battlegroup. There we were, team name <IDK MY BFF JILL>, sitting at Number 1.

I printed off a copy, grabbed some tape and scissors, and in the quiet of the morning marched my way to the kitchen. If he didn't understand before, he had to understand now. I did it, Dad, I thought. I am, officially, the best at what I do. Just like you. And here, see? I have the numbers to prove it.

I had school in an hour. Hadn't slept at all. I rubbed my eyes and examined the refrigerator. This was where everything important got posted — bible verses and unfilled allowance charts and inspirational quotes like, "Who you are speaks so loudly, I cannot hear what you're saying." I found an empty space to hang my achievement and stood back to admire my work. It was beautiful. Who'da thought, Dad? Your son. A professional gamer.

And then I came to a devastating realization. The team sitting at #2 was <your moms a Horde>, and the #5 team was <come honour face>. And all sorts of other team names I always thought were hilarious but knew my dad would never take seriously. Or my mother. Or my siblings, for that matter. So I rummaged around the kitchen and found a black permanent marker, to cross out all the "inappropriate" teams, only to be left with an almost-unreadable sheet edited with thick, black lines.

That's when it hit me. If I was an orthopedic surgeon, running downstairs at 5:30 a.m for a quick gallon of coffee and a small trough of oatmeal before hopping in my six series Beamer to go straighten some fat lady's spine, I wouldn't know what this paper with permanent marker all over it was. So I found another pen, red this time, and drew a really big circle around my team and character's name, and then right next to it wrote, "Exitec = Your son."

But he had three sons! Sure, I was the only one obsessed with World of Warcraft, but still, I wanted there to be absolutely no confusion. I tilted my head, balanced my elbow on the fridge, and proceeded to fill the margins with our story: how we had been playing together for four months straight, how we'd beaten all the best teams, even the ones with professional sponsors, and how maybe soon we'd be offered a sponsorship and start playing in tournaments, and maybe I didn't even need college, Dad! You know how you always said, "Do what you love, and be the best at what you do?" Well Dad, I'm doing it. And I did it by working hard. "Just do it, Cole." I listened to you. I really did. I put my head down and worked as hard as I could and I finally, finally did it. Out of twelve million players, I am standing at the top.

And then footsteps started to move upstairs. His bedroom door opened and I could hear tired, heavy feet dragging across the hall. I looked at the refrigerator and my name, Exitec, circled at the top. I'd worked so hard to get there.

When he landed in the front hallway, I ripped it down. My success crumpled in my hands. He walked into the kitchen and asked what I was doing up so early. I walked towards the garbage and told him I was just finishing some homework.

He asked what I had in my hand.

I told him it was nothing, and threw it away.

Q: So you made it to the top, and then you realized —

A: I realized my achievement would never be enough.

The fact that I was so eager to show him something I had obtained through cheating just goes to show how desperate I was for his approval. It wasn't even about the game. All I wanted was for my dad to look at me like I was worthy of everything he had given me: the big house, the king size bed, the BMW, all the hockey camps, the endless opportunities, anything and everything I could have ever wanted, handed to me on a silver platter. I did the best with what I could. No, I wasn't the star athlete or the captain of the Math team. No, I wasn't the Valedictorian. I was a really, really sick adolescent with stomach aches every day. I was diagnosably depressed. I wasn't eating. I was an insomniac. I had no self-worth. I hated who I was, my body, my face, my smile, my voice, the way I talked, the way I walked, I hated everything about me — except who I was on the Internet. That, I was proud of, because I had built it from nothing. N00b to Gladiator. And all I wanted was for him to look at that and say, "That's pretty impressive. Nice job, Cole."

Q: And when you actually got the Rank 1 title, how did that feel?

A: Well, that's the funny part…

I didn't end up getting the Rank 1 Merciless Gladiator title. The next day, literally 24 hours before Season 2 ended, Frappacino, our Druid, went all emo and decided he didn't want to get Rank 1 by cheating. And I swear to you, to this day I have no idea how this actually happened, but he was the formal "leader" of our 3v3 team, and he decided to disband it.

After I got home from school, Escape and I just sat there in Ventrilo together, speechless. We were both going on zero sleep, since we had stayed up the entire night before win-trading. We had 24 hours to somehow take a team from 1500 to Gladiator, again. And the majority of all the top teams were sitting on their ratings, not playing, because they wanted to make sure they got Gladiator. Back in 2007, you could still get Gladiator in all three brackets: 2v2, 3v3, and 5v5. Escape and I had no choice. We made a 2v2 team and got to work.

And just to give you a better sense of who I was competing with here: Escape was a cokehead living in his mom's basement. He worked at Taco Bell, and stole Internet from his neighbors because he couldn't afford his own. But he was one of the best Rogues I'd ever seen play the game.

When my parents came into my room and saw me in front of my computer that night, a school night, I insisted that I was so far ahead of schedule of everything that I literally had nothing to do. I aced my last two exams. I had finished all my homework. I had worked ahead three chapters in my ACT prep book. I had already practiced the piano. I made up every lie possible so that they would just leave me alone for 24 more hours — that's all I needed.

210

Starting at 3:45 p.m. and ending around 9:00 p.m., with a small break for dinner, Escape and I climbed the 2v2 ladder from 1500 to 2250. I was chugging orange juice, hyped up on sugar. Escape was doing lines of coke between games. And team after team, match after match, we rolled through the competition. I didn't even know what cocaine did as a seventeen year old. All I knew was that Escape played better when he was snorting in the background. Mage/Rogue was the most aggressive 2v2 team composition in the game. You either won in less than 30 seconds, or you lost. You had no healer. You had no real long-term survivability. You either ran in and one-shotted one of the enemy players, or you didn't.

That night, every single game was our best game. We even, near the end, faced off against the Warlock and Shaman from the Alliance 3v3 team we had beaten not four days prior, and the ones currently sitting at Number 1. They were playing 2v2 for fun, since that bracket didn't matter for them, and we smoked them. Rogue/Mage should not beat Warlock/Shaman, and yet we did. Escape and I were so in sync, it felt like we were playing music. We landed a perfect CC chain on the healer, and destroyed the Warlock in a matter of seconds.

As soon as the match was over, we both knew we had hit the top. We were within range to get our Gladiator title, but more importantly, we knew we were the best. We congratulated each other on an incredible season, thanked each other for sticking it out to the very end, and then went to bed. Come morning, we would be Gladiators.

Walking home from school the next day, I couldn't help but reflect on the entire journey. All the different twists and turns I had taken in order to reach the top. It was so clear to me that Success was not a straight shot. It was, by no means, a clear trajectory from point A to point B. I thought about how it had all started with Alex, and how I really just picked up the game because I wanted to make a friend. I thought about how I had decided to start all over and reinvent myself as a Mage. I thought about how I had pushed myself as far as I could go, and then acknowledged that I needed a

211

mentor, someone to teach me. I thought about the investment Cachexic had made, and Sik, and all the hours they had spent with me, making me a better player. I thought about how I had taken the leap to step out of Cachexic's shadow and go my own way. I thought about how many hours I had spent practicing my craft. I thought about how I had passed on so many short-term rewards with the hopes of the long-term pay off. I thought about how I could have spent more time getting into late-night raids and collecting epic, rare items, and how I had invested that time to practice my skills as a player. I thought about how I could have spent more time farming gold and having a "rich character." I thought about how I constantly had to borrow gold from friends just to pay for my repairs and my enchants, how I could have done more quests, collected more mounts, made a fortune off the Auction House, but I took all that time instead and focused it into one bucket: becoming the best Mage in the entire world. I thought about how long I had delayed myself gratification for this moment, this moment of becoming a Gladiator.

I walked up the driveway and into the garage, opened the door that led to the kitchen and set my backpack down on the big fireplace next to the kitchen table. I made my way upstairs and into my bedroom, closed the door and took a seat in my computer chair. I logged into the World of Warcraft and looked at my character. I didn't need to enter the game to see whether or not I had achieved the title — I knew. Deep down, I knew. I, me, Cole, not the character on the screen, Cole, the boy sitting in his computer chair, was a Gladiator.

When I finally hit the Enter key and appeared inside Orgrimmar, my chat box started to flood with messages from other players: congratulating me on my achievement, asking if I wanted to join their arena team for Season 3, etc. Escape messaged me and said congrats, and we reminisced for a few minutes about the past four months together. How many nights we had gone insane trying to figure out how we were going to beat certain teams. How many times we almost got screwed there at the end. How, even though it had been frustrating and exhausting and by no means an easy road, the past four months were some of the best months of our lives. We had left it all on the table, and at the end, there we were, standing at the top.

After enjoying my achievement for ten or fifteen minutes, and responding to other players in chat, I logged off and walked over to my bed, falling into my pillows. I looked up at the ceiling and felt as though I was on the top of the Grand Canyon, looking out at the vastness and wondering, "What else is there for me? How much higher can I go?"

Q: If I were to guess where I think this is all going, this is the perfect segue, isn't it?

A: You already know.

Once I achieved the title of Gladiator, everything I could have ever wanted in the game came barreling towards me.

Players paid me obscene amounts of gold to carry them up the arena rankings. I made more gold the week after I hit Gladiator than I had in the three and a half years of playing World of Warcraft prior, combined. Other players would give me enchants or items I needed for free, hoping that their positive association with me would bring good things for them. Top competitors tried to poach me for their 3v3 teams. I got accepted into any guild I wanted, without question, simply because having a Gladiator in the guild was good publicity. When I would play with other top teams, if I made a mistake in an arena, nobody questioned me or called me out — which used to happen. They would just laugh it off, not wanting to piss off the almighty Gladiator Exitec.

I was treated like a king.

Now, the con to all of this, which is the last part of this story, is how short my reign at the top truly lasted.

As soon as I had the title of Gladiator, I felt like I didn't have to try as hard. Instead of letting my skill speak for me, I kicked back and flaunted my title. I started to get complacent because I had nothing left to prove. I was no longer that hungry kid, determined to hit the top. I had hit the top, and had nowhere else to

213

go.

This was the turning point that led to my downfall.

I hit Gladiator late November, 2007. At the same time, I had just started seeing Rose.

Q: I didn't know her back then. What was she like?

A: She was incredible. We met at the show choir camp my mom taught at every summer, Shooting Spotlights. We were in the high school group together, and she was one of the Big Kid helpers with me that worked with the first through fourth graders in the afternoon. She was a little bit shorter than me, bright green eyes and medium length blonde hair. And she could dance. She was probably the best dancer in our whole group. I found her so attractive. She was just a genuinely nice person. And she was always really nice to me.

We became good friends that summer because we saw each other every day, for four consecutive weeks working this show choir camp. I knew I had no chance with her, because she went to another high school and was dating someone else at the time, so I felt like I could just be myself because I had nothing to lose. I would crack jokes and make her laugh, and when she smiled, I smiled. Her energy was warm, open and friendly. I admired her for being so at ease with life — something I struggled very much with on my own.

Near the end of the summer, we vowed to stay in touch. Like I said, we were just friends — but good friends. She was actually the first real friend I had that was a girl. We texted quite a bit, and even though I was entirely focused on Success in the World of Warcraft, I started to share more and more about myself with her. Some weekends, whenever I wasn't playing 3v3, we would meet up and go to a movie, or I would make the thirty-minute drive and go over to her house to just hang out. She tried setting me up with her friends, but it never worked. It was almost always my fault, a combination of my awkwardness and subsequent unwillingness to sacrifice too much time away from my computer.

Conversely, she started sharing with me a lot more about herself too. Her and her boyfriend had broken up, and she hinted at how he hadn't treated her well. I told her she deserved better, that she was a very special type of person and should find someone who could treat her with love and respect, and she thanked me often for being genuine. I meant every word. I thought the world of her.

As soon as I hit Gladiator though, and I had nothing else to work towards in the game, Rose and I naturally started seeing each other more often. I was willing to spend more time away from my computer, and the more time we spent together the more we realized that we had become best friends — and not just best friends, but practically boyfriend and girlfriend.

She became my Escape, my partner in life. Every single morning, I would wake up early and write her a long text, telling her how much I appreciated her and thought she was the most beautiful girl I had ever seen. Every day at lunch, I would send her another short text, counting down the days until we could see each other again — since we could really only make it work on the weekends. And every night before bed, I would write the longest letter of them all, a text broken up into fifteen different parts, one part poetry, two parts prose, overflowing into her phone with love, all the love I had suppressed in my pursuit for Success now rushing out — and at the same time, begging for her to return the gift and tell me that she loved me too.

Q: Sounds like a combination of butterflies and a coping mechanism, am I right?

A: One hundred percent. It was both.

I loved that girl more than I loved myself — and that was precisely the problem. I would pour, and pour, and pour out how much I loved her, not just so that she knew how I felt, but so that she would return back to me the very thing I was so desperately looking for in my life: Love.

It's just, it was never enough. She would tell me she loved me and it felt like a droplet of water from a leaky faucet — when what I wanted was an ocean.

What I wanted was my parents' love — which I equated with approval.

I can't remember exactly when it happened, but sometime that second semester of my senior year, a perfect storm began to form inside me. Cachexic had returned to the game, as had Sik and the rest of <Loot Crusade>, except nobody really took the World of Warcraft all that seriously anymore — myself included. Sik was starting law school and just sort of playing for fun. <Loot Crusade> as a guild became more of a place for us all to hang out. And Cachexic was attending community college, smoking a lot of weed.

It's hard to say exactly what the lighter fluid was that sparked my initial decision: Maybe I still looked to Cachexic for guidance, trusting in him as a mentor. Maybe I just wanted his approval. Maybe it was the fact that after I had hit Gladiator, I was bored. Maybe it was the day I received my college acceptance letter in the mail from the University of Missouri, my parents, and my whole family really, cheering and hugging me and congratulating me on something that held absolutely no emotional value in my life. I hadn't poured my heart and soul into school, hadn't set the goal of college and worked my ass off to reach the top of that summit. Maybe it was their validation toward something that I didn't want validation for that ignited in me uncontrollable anger. I don't know. I don't know what that "one moment" was that pushed me over the edge, but something did.

I started smoking a lot of weed.

Cachexic walked me through the process, step by step. How to buy a bag. How to empty "the guts" of a Black and Mild. How to roll a blunt. How to smoke it. What it would feel like.

I bought an eighth from a kid in my choir class who I knew smoked. I met him on a side street in our suburb in my BMW and brought it home, the Ziplock bag stinking up my entire bedroom. That night, I pulled it out of my desk, right there in the open, and started to examine the green nuggets. I pulled out a Black and Mild from the pack I'd bought at the gas station, and starting at the top, tearing it apart. I emptied "the guts" into my trashcan, and then licked the edges a bit to open up it up — just like Cachexic had told me. From the Ziplock bag, I picked off tiny little pieces from the green nugget and sprinkled them inside the wrap. Then I rolled it up. Failed. Tried again. Failed. I threw the wrap out and started with a new one. Tried again. Failed. Tried again. I finally ended up with a flattened and jagged blunt, which I figured was smokeable. I did it all right there at my desk, in plain sight. No being sneaky, like I had been for years with the World of Warcraft. No checking down the hall to see whether or not anyone was still awake. No bothering to consider that if I got caught "doing drugs" by my mother or father, I would quite literally be punished in the worst way possible. In fact, it all barely crossed my mind. It was as if I wanted them to walk in and see what I was doing. I wanted them to see my destruction manifesting. That I was coping. That somewhere along the way, I had come to the subconscious realization that if obtaining the title and achieving Success in the World of Warcraft still didn't give me their approval, their love, then what would? Would anything? Could I ever pursue something I loved, and reach Success on my own terms, and receive their love and approval at the same time? Or was I stuck? Either I pursue Success as they formally define it, and compromise myself and what I want to do in life, but receive their love and approval, or pursue what I want and Success on my own terms, but forever be seen as "not enough" and unworthy of their love.

Q: Were you aware of all that at the time?

A: If you want me to be perfectly honest with you, I didn't realize that until I just wrote it down right here, in this book, over ten years later. I always thought I started smoking weed and escaped through substances because I wanted to rebel, and because I hated my parents, and all those things I was told by them and therapists and people looking from the outside who reduced me to being this disobedient teenager with no direction in life. But after many, many years of soul searching, I now realize that I wasn't rebelling for the sake of rebellion. I was so mind-fucked and hurt because on some level, I felt like I had to choose: I either stayed true to myself, and had my parents look down upon me, or I listened to them and became who they wanted me to become, but suppressed my own heart and where I truly wanted to go in life.

Now that I think about it, this is something a lot of people go through, they just go through it later on in life. This happens when you're thirty or forty or fifty, and you look back and you say, "You know, I would have liked to have been a guitarist. But my dad wanted me to go into law — so I became a lawyer." We hear people say that all the time, and yet we think nothing of it. And it's this pursuit, this seeking of parental approval and "love" that drives so many people to "formal Success." These people become esteemed businessmen, doctors, lawyers, CEOs, climb the ladder and end up with the big fancy title at the end and essentially beat the game, and then look back with regret and say, "You know, this wasn't what I really wanted to do in life. My dream was actually something else." That's the saddest thing in the world, to me — and on some level, I learned that as a teenager.

Well, no. I *started* to learn that as a teenager. And then I went through a period of self-destruction where, in all honesty, I didn't know what to do. I didn't know whether I needed to obtain a higher title, a better title, or if I needed to say, "I fucking hate this game," burn my life down, and prove to my parents that it's all bullshit.

I went with the latter.

Q: Yeah, that next year was not healthy — for the both of us. What was it like right before you left home and went off to college?

A: I was a total mess. I got accepted into the University of Missouri, the top journalism school in the country, the plan being to study journalism. My parents were so proud — and I couldn't have cared less. My gaming blog was more popular than ever. GameRiot was in talks with an investment firm about raising money — and they asked me if I would consider being a full-time salaried writer for the website. I wasn't really competing in World of Warcraft anymore, and whenever I would play I was either drunk or high. I would go upstairs to the kitchen, and with my dad in the living room and my mom in the sunroom, I'd grab a big tall glass from the cabinet, walk over to the liquor pantry in the back, pull out a bottle of vodka (wheat), fill up half the glass, and then fill the other half with orange juice and walk right back upstairs to my computer. My parents would come by my bedroom and see me sitting there with my big tall glass of orange juice and think nothing of it, telling me they were going to bed, saying goodnight, not even bothering to pull me off my computer. I'd gotten into college and would be leaving in a few months. I was free to coast and play as much World of Warcraft as I wanted. They were happy.

There was a point my senior year when I was getting drunk or high, usually both, at least four nights a week, laughing hysterically into my headset with the other Gladiators I was playing with. We were all elites, bored out of our minds, sitting at the top of the summit with no other goal to drive us. We played drinking games together where we would all take shots if we lost a match — and sure enough, with each loss we became more and more sloppy, until someone passed out and we had to call it a night.

With the room spinning and my speech slurred, I would pull out my bag of weed and roll myself another blunt, walking downstairs to the backyard to smoke myself into oblivion. I would sit under the stars and look up at the hazy sky, the trees moving in and out of focus, the light of the moon drawing me in like a warm blanket. When I was done, I'd walk back inside and dance with my shadow as we, together, made our way upstairs. With my brand new laptop for college on my lap, curled up in bed, I would write in my journal. I couldn't write blogs like this — and I didn't want to. But I wanted to journal. I wanted to carve my heart out, night after night, and put it on paper. All so I could look at it and ask myself, "What the fuck do you want? What is it you're searching for?"

As the semester finished and summer started, my substance abuse went through the roof. I was smoking every single day. Rose started to get worried. Since she was very popular at her school, she often got invited to parties — and since we had started officially dating, she would bring me too. I would get blackout drunk, every time. So drunk that she would have to walk me to the car, and as we were driving home she would have to pull over so that I could throw up. There were so many nights where we would sit outside my house together, waiting for me to come back to my senses before I walked in and faced my parents. How I went so long without getting caught is a pure reflection of how distant the thought was from my parents' minds. I might have been an aggravating kid, might have spent a little too much time in front of my computer, might not have been the best student, but never did they think I would ever join the ranks of kids that abused substances at such an early age. They trusted me.

Q: You ended up getting caught though, right? Because I remember the day your parents dropped you off at Mizzou and things were not so good.

A: Yup, I eventually got caught. The week before I was supposed to leave for college, my entire life fell apart.

It was a tornado of things, really. First of all, my relationship with my parents was the best it had ever been. Really. They could barely contain their excitement for me, about to spread my wings and go off to college — of course, at the same time they were sad they would be saying goodbye to their baby boy, but still. We barely fought that summer, if at all. I had a beautiful, blonde girlfriend. I was spending more time doing things away from my computer. I was going to attend a massive university. They felt like I was finally "normal."

Second, both Rose and I had come to realize that I would be leaving soon and between us would be six hundred miles. She still had one more year of high school to go. We talked a lot about it, and vowed to stay together. I told her I wanted to marry her. I said, in a voice of poetry, that in the grand scheme of things this one year apart would be nothing compared to a lifetime together. I still remember the night I told her that. At the time, it seemed so beautiful. So perfect. It was just a year — and then hopefully she would attend the University of Missouri too.

220

Third, my mom had been doing a lot of research about food and her own stomach issues, and had suggested that I go on a gluten-free diet. In the beginning, I was extremely opposed — I couldn't imagine a life without pizza or muffins or chocolate cake. But at some point, enough was enough. The week before I was supposed to leave for school, I ate one dinner that was completely gluten free: salmon, brown rice, and steamed broccoli. I left the table feeling like a million dollars. I wasn't rushing for the bathroom. I wasn't clutching my stomach in pain. It was as if, in an instant, my chains had been released and I was free to roam the world as I pleased. My sentence in the bathroom was complete.

Our last week of summer was to be spent, as a family, up at our favorite vacation spot in the world: a tiny cabin in northern Wisconsin, part of a private club. My father had spent years trying to be accepted, and it became family tradition for us to drive eight hours to this magical place in the middle of nowhere, turning off this small dirt road and onto eighty acres of private property, six lakes, twelve cabins for rent, and a master lodge with a full kitchen staff. It was not intended to be a flashy, Presidential-Suite-in-Hawaii type of vacation. It was where we went, as a family, to detach from the world and enjoy each other's company.

This year, I would be bringing Rose. She had become part of our collective, practically a sister to Brooke, Thomas, and Donald. My whole family loved her. My mother thought she was everything I needed and more. My father constantly reminded me that I had "found a keeper." My sister and her got along great. And Thomas and Donald, on the cusp of approaching puberty themselves, I'm sure looked at her and wondered how they could grow up and find someone like her too. She really was the perfect girlfriend a teenage boy could ever have.

Well, the day before we left for vacation, my three siblings begged and pleaded to help me pack for college. They were so sad to see their older brother go, and wanted to be part of the process. For the first time in my life, I really did feel like "the older brother." Someone they could look up to. So I said sure, you can help me pack, and invited them into my room.

221

Thomas, just wanting to help, opened the drawer to my desk and saw my bag of weed and my brand new yellow bowl — my first real purchase as a seasoned smoker. As soon as he opened the drawer, he looked up at me, not sure what to do, and I knew. I knew it was all over. He was still so young — he was only twelve. He got scared and later that day told my dad. My dad told my mom. My mom's entire world crumbled, her son "a drug addict." And the rest was history.

For the entire eight-hour drive up to Wisconsin, nobody talked to me. Nobody acknowledged me. Nobody wanted anything to do with me. As soon as we pulled up to our cabin, my father excused everyone to our boat, Rose included, and called me into the bedroom and screamed at me like I had never been screamed at in my entire life. He started crying, asking me, and himself, where he had gone wrong. What he possibly could have done to deserve me hurting him like this. He told me I had destroyed the family, destroyed my mother and him and their trust in me. He said I didn't deserve to go to college. That I didn't deserve anything he had worked so hard for in life and handed to me on a silver platter. He threatened to call the cops and send me to jail, if that's what it took to get me in line. And all I could do was sit there, numb — I didn't feel a thing. I was dead to him, and to myself, somewhere within me convinced that if my acquisition of a Title was not enough to warrant their love, then there was no point in playing the game anymore. I hated the game. I never wanted to play the game ever again — this game of Success. I wanted to ruin the game. I wanted to destroy the game. I wanted to prove, to them and to the world, that chasing the mountain peak of Success all for the high of approval would never fulfill the deep and empty longing within for true love.

So I decided if self-destruction was part of that journey, then so be it. I would throw it all away. I would make it all crumble. I would tear down my entire life until I had nothing, nothing left at all, just to prove the worthlessness of The Game.

Q: But you still went to Mizzou. How?

A: I made a few half-hearted promises that I would never

222

smoke again. That I was sorry. That I didn't mean to. It was all lies. Lies, to them and to myself. For whatever reason, they decided to let me go. I promised and promised I would never do it again, but deep down I knew. I was in such a horrible place emotionally that all I wanted to do was escape. I wanted to escape from my family and the never-ending tornado of conflict. I wanted to escape from the pain I was going to feel living six hundred miles away from Rose, the only person who I felt truly loved me. I even wanted to escape from the World of Warcraft, the game no longer satisfying this belief in me that Success would fill the void of love.

I'm sure you remember the day when my parents dropped me off at the dorm. They hugged me how I imagine an intern at a hospital hugs a diseased patient — at a distance, withdrawn, emotionally detached. My mother started crying, right there in the doorway. She was in total conflict: half of her not yet ready to let go of her first born son, the other half furious and torn apart that I had succumbed to the one thing she feared the most. My father was completely emotionally absent, standing off to the side, disappointed and heartbroken. He was about to shell out thousands upon thousands of dollars for a college education to a boy who, in all honesty, didn't give a shit and took great pride in throwing it back in his face. I'm not sure if we even hugged goodbye. He just made me promise him, one more time, that I would never smoke again.

When they walked out of the door and down the hallway, I remember peeking out and looking at them from afar before shutting the door.

Finally, I was out of the house.

Finally, I was free.

And in that moment, I had never felt so alone and so destroyed and so sad in my entire life.

Q: And this is where Book II starts?

A: This is where Book II starts.

CPSIA information can be obtained
at www.ICGtesting.com
Printed in the USA
LVOW03s1737141217
559733LV00014B/1531/P